quick & clever handmade cards

Julie Hickey

David & Charles

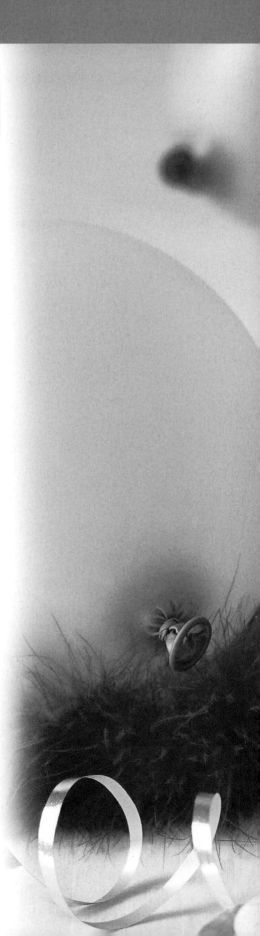

To Mervyn, Matthew, Owen, Mum, Dad, Shine
and to the memory of Laurie.

A DAVID & CHARLES BOOK

First published in the UK in 2004
Reprinfed 2004
Copyright © Julie Hickey 2004

Distributed in North America
by F&W Publications, Inc.
4700 East Galbraith Road
Cincinnati, OH 45236
1-800-289-0963

ISBN 0 7153 1660 5 paperback
ISBN 0 7153 1658 3 hardback

Printed in Singapore by KHL Printing Co Pte Ltd
for David & Charles
Brunel House   Newton Abbot   Devon

Commissioning Editor Fiona Eaton
Desk Editor Jennifer Proverbs
Executive Art Editor Ali Myer
Designer Lisa Forrester
Production Controller Jen Campbell
Photographer Ginette Chapman

Visit our website at www.davidandcharles.co.uk

David & Charles books are available from all good bookshops; alternatively you can contact our Orderline on (0)1626 334555 or write to us at FREEPOST EX2 110, David & Charles Direct, Newton Abbot, TQ12 4ZZ (no stamp required UK mainland).

The author and publisher have made every effort to ensure that all the instructions in this book are accurate and safe, and therefore cannot accept liability for any resulting injury, damage or loss to persons or property however it may arise.

Contents

Introduction

Creating and giving handmade cards means so much more than just buying a mass-produced one – and with a few clever techniques you can make something really eye-catching in no time at all. The person receiving the card feels extra-special, and the act of making the card is both therapeutic and rewarding.

I have always loved card and paper: the joy of looking at a pile of card in all the colours of the rainbow or the tactile pleasure of stroking card and paper, understanding its texture and weight. When buying special card, I always buy two sheets so that I can use one and still have one to get out and look at now and again! I am also a hoarder, like most crafters, and I collect everything that I think can be used to embellish a card. The wrappers from sweets and chocolates; leaves from country walks; shells from the beach and unusual wrapping paper are just a few of the countless possibilities.

I have no formal art training. I think I get my eye for colour from my mum, who has a talent for flower arranging and excellent clothes sense. I can't draw – but haven't let this stop me. I have had many happy years of rubber stamping, the stamps doing the drawing for me, giving me free reign to colour the design. It just goes to show that if you have a passion for something, you can do it.

Card making is really the art of putting things together to create mini-designs. Inspiration for these designs is all around us: magazines, crockery, serviettes, a garden or a trip to the seaside. In this book I explain how to combine all sorts of materials to produce creative and fun results, and show you many quick and clever techniques for achieving wonderful cards for every occasion. From birthdays to anniversaries, congratulations to thank you cards.

Whenever I demonstrate around the country I am asked if I have a book to help clients remember all the ideas I have shown them. Well here it is, many creative ideas and quick tips waiting to be used. Change the cards in anyway you want – make them yours. Use the ideas and skills to start your creativity flowing. Take bits from different cards and put them together in your own way. I hope they inspire you and act as a springboard for creating new ideas of your own.

Crafting above all should be fun. Enjoy the journey of creating something special for the important people in your life and you will find that the effort put into making a handmade card makes it a treasured keepsake. When you realize how easily you can produce something really memorable I hope you will be inspired to pick up your craft tools and create.

How to use this book

The book is divided into three sections. The front of the book introduces practical and design basics to get you started. I list the essential tools and materials you need for card making, along with some more specialized equipment I have acquired over the years. Some basic techniques are explained along with ideas on design and colour. If you are interested in selling your cards, I divulge a few trade secrets and if you want to mass-produce your own cards for a special occasion such as a wedding, I outline a simple plan of campaign.

The middle section contains step-by-step instructions for making quick and clever cards for all occasions. Each project lists all the materials you need with photographs and instructions to help you achieve superb end-results. Simple changes to a card create a whole new look, and I have included variation ideas for each project.

Gallery pages at the back of the book present a wealth of inspirational card ideas and a selection of messages and sayings to suit every occasion.

Equipment

I have items in my workbox that I use all the time when I'm making cards – and other bits and pieces that I use just occasionally. It is worth assembling a basic tool kit, as this is the equipment you will use again and again. Tools that you need only occasionally for a special technique can be acquired gradually, when you are confident you are going to be making more cards. I have built my workbox up over a number of years, and enjoy adding to it frequently!

quick and clever *

*　It is a good idea to keep your equipment organized so you can lay your hands on what you need – when you need it. I use a large tool box; a smaller tool box or even a shoe box would be suitable as you start to build up your supplies.

Basic Tool Kit

With each project in this book I have listed all the specific materials you need; in addition you may need some of the items from this basic tool kit.

Cutting mat The best surface for cutting on with a craft knife as cut marks seal back up. Also a firm surface to rubber stamp on.

Craft knife Use to cut out awkward shapes, help stick small stickers on to cards and trim bits down. Always have a sharp blade in the knife.

Metal ruler For cutting straight lines with a craft knife.

Plastic ruler For measuring card and paper.

Set square (not shown) Use to align work centrally on cards. There is a centre '0' position with centimetre or inch markings working out from this point to the left and right. Mark the centre of your card. Position the centre '0' position of the set square on this mark and use the measurements on either side to position different elements of the card precisely.

Double-sided tape Perfect for mounting card on to card.

Pencil Used to trace patterns, mark measurements and countless other little jobs.

Eraser Use a plastic eraser that won't leave marks on the card.

Scissors Fine pointed scissors will enable you to get right into the nooks and crannies. Soft foam handles are very comfortable to use.

Tracing paper Use to trace off patterns provided at the back of the book (see pages 100–102).

Bone folder (right) This is a vital piece of equipment for the card maker as it creates perfect creases and professional-looking cards.

Decorative Tools

Inkpads Use a black permanent inkpad for stamping out designs. This ink will not smudge even if you apply water to watercolour pencils. Pearlescent inkpads are good for sponging and stamping backgrounds on cards.

Cosmetic sponges Use to apply ink from the inkpads on to paper or card.

Paintbrush Use inkpads and a wet paintbrush to add colour to your cards, or use the paintbrush with watercolour pencils.

Self seal bags Keep tiny no hole glass beads in self seal bags, then put the whole card inside the bag, rub the beads on to the sticky area, tip the excess back into the bag and seal them up ready to be used next time.

quick and clever

∗ Store inkpads upside down so the ink remains at the surface and the pad is moist and ready to be used.

For Manipulating Material

Embossing tool Essential for scoring cards (see page 14). Also used to trace patterns on to copper sheet (see Father's Day Metallic Card, page 54).

Foam sheet When embossing metal use a foam sheet to work on.

Heat Tool This is specially designed for crafting, and produces a very intense heat. Use it to heat copper metal that changes colour when warmed and to heat shrink plastic (see Kiddie Cat Birthday, page 30).

Heat-resistant chopping board You need a heat-resistant work surface when using a heat tool to heat copper metal or shrink plastic.

Adhesives

Adhesive foam pads
These pads are adhesive on both sides – simply remove the backing paper and stick to your card. They come in different sizes and are great for achieving a raised effect when attaching items to your card.

Double-sided adhesive paper
Punch out shapes (see near right) then stick foil, glitter or beads to them. Alternatively, use as a backing for a cut-away panel and add a background (see Glittering Mosaic Thank You, page 58).

Glue pen
These pens have a nice fine nib so they are ideal for sticking tiny shapes to cards.

All purpose sticky craft glue
A tacky craft glue that is used for many different craft applications; from wood to metal, fabric to card and paper. It is a very thick white glue that dries clear. Use for adding charms, flat back crystals or wire to cards.

Super glue
A quick drying, strong glue used to stick items to cards.

Spray adhesive
Glue in a spray can. Excellent for sticking fine, handmade papers and serviettes to card. Always read the instructions on the can before using, and use in a well-ventilated room, or outside.

Cardboard box
Spray glue into a cardboard box to avoid the glue going everywhere. The box remains sticky and will then hold tiny items in place while applying glue to them.

Xyron machine
An excellent tool for applying self-adhesive to the back of artwork – whatever the shape the machine only applies glue where there is somewhere for it to stick to. Turn the handle and out comes your self-adhesive artwork, use the guillotine on the back of the machine to cut it off. Remove the film covering then peel back the backing paper from the artwork and it is ready to use (see pictures, top right). Xyron machines are available in different sizes from 2.5cm (1in) wide to A4 (US letter).

quick and clever

You can change the cartridge of the Xyron (above right) and apply magnets to the back of your work, or you can even laminate it.

Trimming and Punching

Hole punch
Use to create holes in paper, card, foil or shrink plastic.

Paper trimmer
Use to cut card and paper to size. You can also use it as a guide when scoring cards and for making sure that letters or a message have been applied in a straight line.

Small and large guillotine
For cutting card, paper and metal to size.

Eyelet punch, hammer and setter tool
(right) When adding eyelets to a card you will need the punch to create the hole in your card, put the eyelet in the hole, turn the card over and then use the setter tool and a hammer to flatten the eyelet.

Paper and Card

There are so many different coloured cards and papers on the market; you can have any colour of the rainbow in a variety of finishes. What you choose will depend on the use you are putting the card or paper to – if you are choosing card to make the basis of the greetings card, then the weight and colour are of prime importance. If you are looking for card or paper to use as embellishments then you can take your pick from the many different styles that are now available.

Look out for...

Finishes
Paper and card come with pearlized finishes, different metallic finishes and even shimmery card that changes colour as you move it. A touch of shimmer can really make a card special (see Woven Wedding Anniversary, page 50).

Textures
Paper and card comes in an array of textures from smooth to hammered; striped and even animal skin textures. Texture will add interest to your card.

Patterns
Patterned papers are very popular and come with every design you could ever think of. Use them as a background or cut out individual motifs and use as an embellishment. They are suitable for so many different uses and occasions.

Paper vellum
This is a tough, translucent craft material available in a variety of colours, patterns and finishes. You can even get beautiful embossed vellums. It is not true vellum, which is a parchment made from calfskin and is extremely expensive. You can put paper vellum through your home computer and print special messages and greetings on it to make great invitations or inserts for your cards (see Girlie Birthday Card, page 26).

Mulberry paper
There are lots of fibres in this lovely handmade paper. Use a wet paintbrush to mark where you want to tear the paper, then tease the dampened fibres apart to create a lovely wispy edge.

Left and top centre: pearlized pre-scored blanks shown in a range of colours and textures.

mottled card

patterned paper vellum

patterned paper vellum

mulberry paper

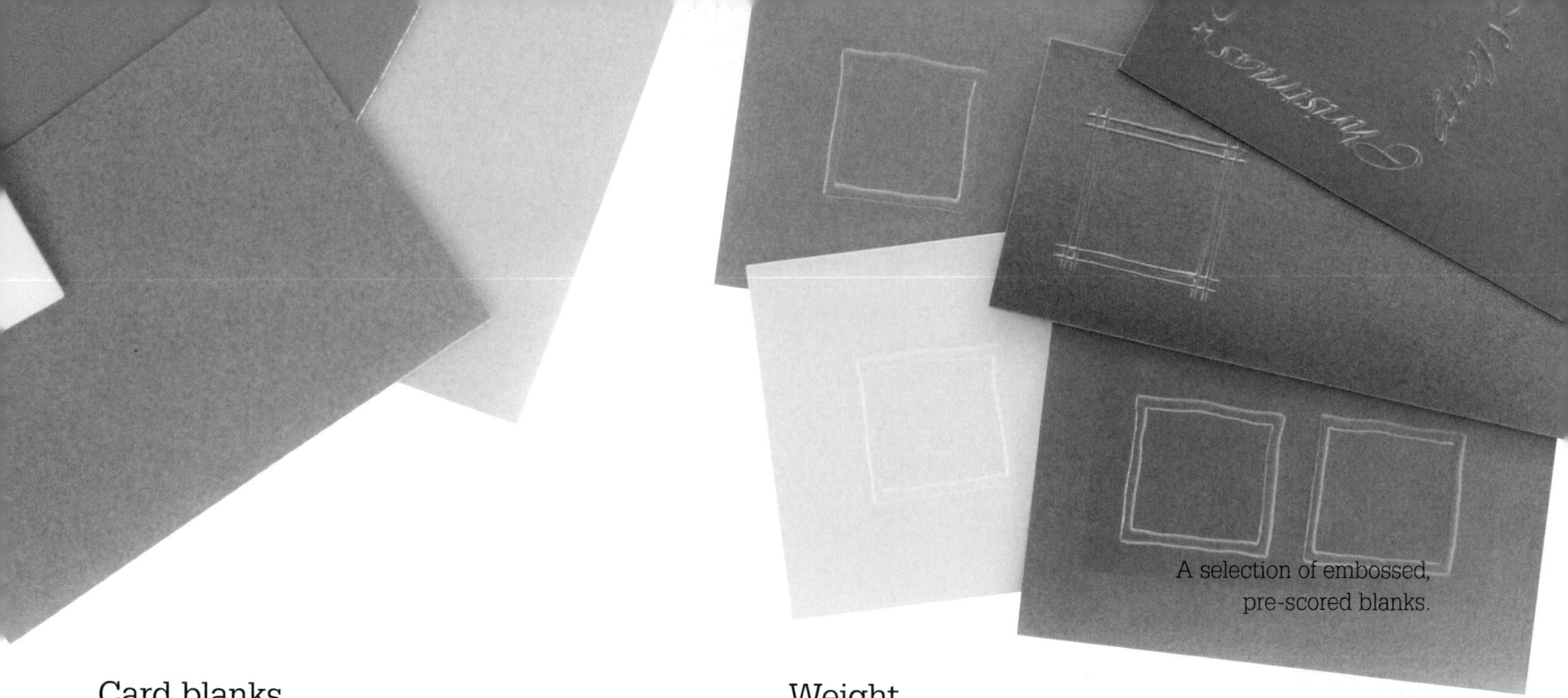

A selection of embossed, pre-scored blanks.

Card blanks

Card blanks are scored cards produced mechanically. They are more expensive than buying card and scoring and folding it yourself, but you may decide they are worth the money for the crisp, clean look they produce. They are available in many different shapes and sizes and in different finishes: from plain to pearlized, patterned and textured. You can buy cards with all sorts of different borders from postage stamp to floral and hearts – just about anything you can think of.

Aperture cards

Aperture cards have small shapes cut out of them, ideal for displaying small embellishments. Blanks come with a range of different shaped apertures in all sorts of sizes, from circles and squares to ovals and rectangles. Some companies produce cards with Christmas tree or heart-shaped apertures. If you can't find exactly what you want, contact a card company and tell them about your idea. If they like it, and think it will sell well, they may produce it.

Blank cards are available with ready-cut apertures in all shapes and sizes.

Weight

The weight of the card and paper you choose is very important. You need to know the GSM: the thickness of the card. A good average weight is 260gsm, but be aware that different colours give different weights; some colour pigments are heavier than others. I find the best way is to feel the card, you can tell if it feels thick enough to stand up when you have attached decorations, or if it is going to bend and bow. Buy the best quality card you can afford – this will produce a professional result.

Paper Sizes

There are standard sizes that are useful to know when buying card blanks or card for cutting and scoring your own cards. The most common size is A5 – two A5 cards can be cut and folded from one sheet of A4 (US letter). In the card trade A5 is often referred to as C6, which is the size of envelopes used for the folded A5 card.

name of card	size of card
A4 (US letter)	21 x 29.5cm (8¼ x 11⅝in)
A5 – or C6 (half A4)	14.8 x 21cm (5¾ x 8¼in)
A6 (half A5)	10.5 x 14.8cm (4⅛ x 5¾in)

Square Cards

I use two standard size square cards 12cm (4¾in) and 14.8cm (5¾in). Both of them can be cut from a single sheet of A4 (US letter). They are also standard sizes for shop bought blanks.

square card size	made from
12cm (4¾in) square	24 x 12cm (9½ x 4¾in) scored and folded
14.8cm (5¾in) square	29.5 x 14.8cm (11⅝ x 5¾in) scored and folded

Embellishments

I have used countless different items to decorate cards with over the years. As well as bought items, there are many things around us that can be adapted: flowers, leaves, colourful papers, magazine pages and more. However, there are some embellishments I return to again and again. I have used them to create the cards in this book and listed them below so you can start to assemble a collection of useful decorations.

Stickers

Peel off stickers There are thousands of sticker designs including words and messages, and they come in as many different colours as you can think of. The sticker gives an embossed effect to the image and it quite simply peels off a sheet and sticks to your card. You can also get clear sticky squares. These are either completely clear or the squares have a gold or silver border to them. They are perfect for mounting small embellishments (see Mother's Day Posy, page 82).

Peel off eyelet stickers and metal eyelets Peel off eyelet stickers come in a variety of colours and they are purely decorative. Metal eyelets can be used with the eyelet punch and setter tool (see page 9) to attach two pieces of card or paper together. They come in hundreds of colours and different shapes.

Decorative Adhesives

Glitter glue Ultra fine glitter and glue mixed together, this comes in a bottle with a lovely fine nozzle. Shake the bottle so that the glue is at the nozzle end and then squeeze very gently. It comes in lots of colours but rhinestone is my favourite, as it is translucent and lets the colour underneath shine through the sparkle.

Dimensional glue This stays raised once it is dry and comes in many colours and in a variety of finishes: glitter, slick and pearl. Use a cocktail stick or paper-pricking tool to apply to tiny flat-back crystals, charms or wire.

Jewels, Beads and Other Ornaments

Flat back crystals Come in all different sizes and wonderful colours. Stick to cards using either an all purpose sticky craft glue or dimensional glue. Place in the centre of flowers, or use to add sparkle to a card.

Seed beads Small beads that can be threaded on to different threads or wire, sewn or stuck to cards. They come in hundreds of colours and several different sizes.

Bugle beads Long tube beads that can be threaded on to something or stuck to card.

Tiny no hole glass beads Incredibly small glass beads with no holes in them. They can be applied to adhesive paper or stuck to cards with glue. They come in a huge variety of colours and in different sizes too. Finer beads give a very professional finish to cards.

Buttons All shapes and sizes of buttons are available and you can find decorative buttons without the attachment used for sewing them on to fabric, so they can be easily mounted. Use an all purpose sticky craft glue, dimensional glue or adhesive foam pads to stick them to card.

Pegs Small decorative pegs can be used to attach other embellishments to cards (see Congratulations On Your Baby, page 62). Find them in stationers or craft shops.

Metal embellishments These are domed metallic shapes that come in various shapes, such as hearts, squares and circles, in lots of different colours. Use dimensional glue to stick them to card.

Pressed flowers Dried flowers that have been pressed in a special way to ensure they keep their bright colours.

Threads and Wire

Ribbon There are some amazing ribbons available and they can really add that finishing touch to a card.

Metallic thread Use with seed and bugle beads and to attach two cards together.

Wire Comes in different gauges, the higher the number the thinner the wire.

Embroidery thread Use to attach buttons to cards or for decorative effect. The thread is made up of six strands, which can be separated out so you can use single threads or two or three together.

Cotton string Can work well for attaching tags or tying cards together.

Miscellaneous

Punches Come in many different motifs and sizes to punch paper and lightweight card. Use them to create panel designs, stencils, decorative tags and many other quick and clever designs.

Rubber stamps A great way to decorate a card if you can't draw. There are thousands of designs available and many different ways to use them to create quick designs.

Watercolour pencils Excellent for adding colour to detailed designs. Add water to create a painted effect.

Ultra-fine glitter Ultra-fine glitter and glass mixed together: available in several colours. This is a translucent product so you can see through the glitter if you apply it over a stamped motif.

Copper metal sheet Pure copper metal that can be heated, embossed, cut, shaped, punched and hammered and made into embellishments for your cards. Only pure copper metal will change colour when heated.

Gel pen These pens will dry on plastic, so use on shrink plastic buttons if you want to colour them in.

Craft shops stock a vast array of colourful items that can be used to create and embellish handmade cards: glues and glitter; punches and coloured pencils; ribbons and beads – you can have fun buying them as well as using them.

Basic Techniques

Here are some simple techniques that will ensure you produce professional-looking cards in next to no time. Pre-scored and folded card blanks, which are manufactured by machinery, are really the very best quality, but can work out expensive if you are making a lot of cards. Many card crafters prefer to buy their own card and cut it to size. Follow these simple instructions for cutting, scoring and folding professional-looking cards; positioning and applying embellishments with double-sided tape; and making card inserts for adding a special message.

Cutting and Folding Your Own Cards

By following these basic techniques when folding card, you will end up with a clean, crisp looking fold on both the inside and outside of all your cards.

Step one

Measure half the length of an A4 (US letter) card, and cut to size with a paper trimmer or using a metal ruler and craft knife on a cutting mat. You now have two A5 cards.

Step two

Measure half the length of one of the A5 cards, and mark the card. Place in the paper trimmer lining the mark up with the groove that cuts the card. Starting at the top, pull an embossing tool down the groove to score the card. Or use a ruler with a bone folder held in an upright position.

Step three

Fold the card, aligning the edges and use a bone folder held flat to carefully flatten the crease.

'valley' fold

quick and clever

❋ The indent on the crease is known as the 'valley' and the bulbous part is known as the 'mountain'. The 'valley' is always on the outside of your card and the 'mountain' is always on the inside. ❋

'mountain' fold

Positioning Design Elements

It can be tricky to position some elements correctly on a card, and I have spoilt many cards with a lopsided finish! However, I was shown this technique for using double-sided tape by a print finisher – it allows you to move the element around and reposition it until you have it perfectly placed, then stick it down.

Step one

Attach double-sided tape to the edges of the element to be stuck to the main card. Then pull back just enough backing paper so that you can see the paper tabs from the front of the card.

Step two

Position the element on your card, moving it around until you are completely happy with the position. (If all the backing paper is removed you only get one go at positioning.) Firm down where the tape is exposed.

Step three

Carefully hold the element in the centre and pull the paper tabs off completely. Firm down on the card.

Making Inserts

If you have added eyelets (see New Home Celebration, page 34) or ribbons to the front of your card, (and for some aperture cards), you may wish to hide what is visible on the inside of the card. You may also want to write special messages or verses in your cards using a computer or special stamp. Inserts are a great way to do both of these. (Remember to print the message from the computer before cutting the paper to fit the card.) For ideas on messages to fit all occasions see page 98.

Colour and texture

Choose paper for your insert that will complement the card and the occasion. You may want to pick a colour to match your card, or achieve a subtle or bold contrast. Parchment-effect paper with a faint pattern gives a fantastic finish, and comes in many different colours. You can print on to vellum, which is available in many different colours, flecked with gold or silver, in an iridescent finish, and even pearlized – all perfect for a special occasion such as a wedding (see pages 22–23).

Embellishment

Use fancy-edged scissors to give added interest to your insert, or apply a gold, silver or coloured pen to the edge, linking it to the card's main colour theme. You don't want the insert to detract from the impact of the card design, so subtle decoration should suffice.

Attaching the insert

To attach the insert with double-sided tape, first cut the insert paper 6mm (¼in) smaller than the card all the way round. Fold in half and crease using a bone folder (see page 14). Apply double-sided tape to the back of the folded insert (see picture left) then place the insert into the folded card. Open the card from the back so that you can see the double-sided tape and remove the backing paper. Shut the card, firming down along the crease of the card.

Alternatively, tie the card and insert together at the centre-fold using ribbon, thread or string decorated with beads, or punch two holes in the fold, thread ribbon through and tie.

Making Envelopes

If you have an unusual size card, or want to create envelopes from papers that match your card, you will need to make your own envelopes. Always use paper – about 120gsm is about the right weight to score and fold for a professional finish. A good quality paper will also protect your creations if you are sending them by post.

Choosing paper

As with inserts, the colour of the envelope can tone or contrast with the card. Patterned papers make fantastic envelopes, or try magazine pages that match the occasion you are marking. Bright and colourful comics are great for children's envelopes, while pages taken from wedding magazines, women's magazines, hobby magazines and many other publications also make great envelopes. It may be a particular picture or theme that matches the card, or a more abstract shape or colour scheme that appeals.

Embellishments

You can rubber stamp your paper to match the design on the card, then make the envelope. Alternatively, look at the techniques and motifs used on the card, then use these to embellish the envelope. A fast way to add a 'lining' to the inside of an envelope is to rubber stamp a pattern on to the wrong side of the paper before you cut out the envelope shape.

Pick a theme from your card to embellish an accompanying envelope for impressive presentation.

Decorate the inside of your envelope by adding a pattern to the back of the paper before cutting it out.

Address labels

You will need a plain address label to ensure the name and address are legible on a patterned envelope. Make your own unique labels by cutting out different shapes from plain address labels, or cut them from coloured paper and run them through a Xyron machine to add an adhesive backing (see page 9). Continue the theme of the card with balloon shapes for birthday cards, hearts for weddings or anniversaries, snowmen for Christmas, and so on.

Making a Template and Envelopes

Before you make your envelope you will need to make a template. I use photocopy paper to create a template, marking the size of the card it fits, the fold line and where to glue. Then I keep it so that I can use it again and again.

Step one

Take a sheet of A4 or A3 paper, depending on the size of your card, and lay the card on top of it – allowing more space at the top than the bottom. Fold the bottom up and the top down, then fold in the sides. Press firmly along the folds to create strong creases.

Step two

Unfold all four sides of the paper. You should be able to see clearly the dimensions of your card, along the folds. Use a pencil and ruler to mark the shape of the side flaps. Do the same for the bottom and top flaps, remembering the top flap must cover the side flaps and overlap the bottom. Trim your template to size.

quick & clever

Christmas wrapping paper is an easy way to make envelopes for Christmas cards – and economical too! Look at other styles of wrapping paper you may have around the house for different occasions.

Sealing your envelope

Transfer your template to your chosen envelope material. Fold in the bottom and side flaps, then glue the bottom flap to the side flaps and leave to dry. To seal the envelope, apply glue to the edges of the top flap, stick down and leave to dry. Ensure the envelope is sealed firmly and will not come apart when it is handled. This is especially important if you are posting your card.

quick and clever

Make sure the top flap is deep enough to allow you to seal the envelope without the glue touching the card inside.

Design and Layout

The designs you choose for your cards are highly personal, and will of course take into account your own taste, the recipient, and the materials and embellishments available to you. However, I have a few guidelines that will get you started.

Planning

The occasion for which you are making the card will often dictate the elements you use. Match the card to the person you are sending it to: what are their passions? Do they have a favourite colour? What might surprise them? The answers and ideas you come up with will help you to decide what to put on their card. When you have a theme for the card, you can then make choices around colour and composition.

For a bright vibrant feel, shiny card will look great. Mirror card, a highly glossy card, is ideal. Charms, glitter and other sparkly embellishments also pack a punch. For a softer, muted look use a matt card layered with matt or handmade paper. Add dimension to your cards by layering different materials or sticking elements on using adhesive foam pads to give them extra lift.

Experiment with colours and textures, and look through the book for inspiration and ideas. Once you are happy with your selection of embellishments, you can start putting your card together.

Assembling the design

Play around with the different elements you are using until you have a layout and design that are pleasing to your eye. A set square will help you to position design elements – use the markings to help you measure the gaps between each element accurately (see page 7). Bad spacing will give an amateur finish to your cards. When you are happy with the positioning, stick your embellishments down.

The occasion and the hobbies and likes of the recipient will help you choose a theme for their card.

Design Tips

It is easy to create eye-pleasing card designs if you follow these quick tips on how to position different elements. Experiment with your own cards and embellishments to find out what works for you.

♥ When adding a row of elements to a card, it is often a good idea to work in odd numbers, as these tend to be more pleasing to the eye. An A5 or C6 card or a long, thin card looks great with three elements on it.

♥ A square card looks fabulous with four elements grouped together. Experiment with different and identical images to see the effects you can achieve.

♥ Four elements work well on rectangular cards, but it is best to group them together to make one large design (left).

♥ Just one element on the front of a rectangular card is very eye-catching. Position it so that the border around the element is roughly even at the top and the sides (left).

If the gaps are too big, the design won't look balanced and elements appear unrelated (right). Smaller gaps give more cohesion and impact.

One element placed right in the middle of a rectangular card will tend to get lost (right).

♥ One element placed centrally on a square card gives a chic, minimalist look that still has impact. This fast approach is especially effective if you are making a production line of cards (see page 22).

♥ Layering card or paper can totally change the look of your cards. Mounting an element on to card or paper before sticking it in place can lift the whole look. I tend to pick a colour that is dominant in the element or card or a similar tone.

Choosing Colour

Colour is a very important part of your card and can make all the difference to the final effect. By changing the colour you can go from soft, subtle and sophisticated to bright and funky. Although I have no formal art training, I have a naturally good sense of colour and a feel for what works together and what doesn't – and a lot of this is personal choice and preference. If you feel nervous about choosing colours to combine on your cards, look at the colour wheel, then read on for some easy hints and tips for choosing colour.

The colour wheel

The colour wheel will help you to decide which colours work together most effectively, as it shows the primary, secondary and tertiary colours. Primary colours are red, blue and yellow. Secondary colours are the result of mixing two of the three primary colours together: green from blue and yellow; orange from red and yellow; and purple from red and blue. When you start to mix the primary colours with the secondary colours you get tertiary colours such as aqua, puce and lime.

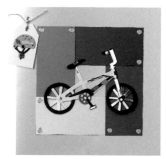

Bright or subtle?

If you want your cards to have really colourful impact, choose colours that are opposite one another on the wheel – red and green, blue and orange, and purple and yellow. These are called complementary colours and will work together to give bold and vibrant results. If you are after something a little softer and gentler on the eye then you need to use colours that are next to each other on the wheel, known as analogous colours.

Cool or warm?

The choice of cool or warm colours has an impact on the feel of a card. The colours on the wheel from red, clockwise round to green are known as warm colours. Aqua round to puce are cool colours. Match gold or copper with warm colours and silver tones with cool colours.

quick & clever

Don't try to use too many colours together. In fact, just one colour in different shades can look fabulous, and is a quick way to vary the look.

What's the occasion?

When designing a card for a specific occasion, certain colours spring to mind. Gold, yellow and cream for a golden wedding anniversary, or deep red and ivory for a Valentine's day or ruby wedding anniversary card. The time of year can influence choice as well: cards featuring shades of copper, gold, deep green and rich reds are ideal for friends who celebrate their birthdays in the autumn or winter.

Fresh citrus colours look great for spring and summer – a combination of yellows, limes and oranges looks fresh and zingy. Don't be frightened to use unusual colour combinations – pinks, oranges and purples look fabulous together, and lime and purple make an unusual but effective partnership for cards that are fast but full of impact for any occasion.

Producing Cards in Bulk

You can save yourself a lot of money by making invitation cards in bulk. Wedding stationery in particular can be very expensive, and you have all the fun of designing it and making it very personal to you and your future partner. Also think how much more the invitations will mean to everyone lucky enough to receive one, as you have invested your time and energy in making it.

It's nice to personalize cards for parties as well — a ruby or golden wedding anniversary invitation designed around the appropriate colours, or cards for a themed party such as 1970s glam or spooky Hallowe'en. A Christening, change of address, new baby — all may warrant a special card announcement.

With a little time spent planning your stationery (whether it is for 10 or 100 people!) and following a few simple rules, you will soon be putting those cards in the post box. Remember to have lots of fun whilst you make them, and enlist the help of family and friends to help share the load.

To follow are my top tips for creating a wedding invitation by production line. I have created a selection of simple but stunning cards to give you some design ideas. Each design is based around a simple heart motif, but just see how many variations on the theme there are! Each one as fast and fun as the last — ideal for a quick and easy production line. (See Wedding Gallery pages 90–91 for more super and speedy examples).

A heart motif design is ideal for a wedding invitation – keep your design simple as you will be producing a large number of the same card.

quick and clever

If you are feeling ambitious, the wedding cards, evening invitations, order of service and thank you cards can have the same design on the front, with different words inside. Reception seating cards have a smaller version of the design on the left-hand side, leaving room for the name on the right.

Creating the design

Plan the design you want on your invitations. Whatever you decide, keep the design simple as you have several to make. Tie in the colour of your bouquet or bridesmaid dresses if you can, but don't worry too much about matching the colour exactly as no one will hold his or her invitation up against the dresses on the big day. The same tone or very close will be fine. Make up a dummy card, then you can assess what materials you will need, in what order you will work with them, and how you can simplify the job.

Selecting the card stock

Pre-scored and folded cards are ideal for production line assembly such as wedding invitations. You want them to look as professional as possible and these will give you the look. They will also save time – if you cut, score and fold your own cards you will need to add on several days' worth of labour.

When buying your card stock, shop around and get catalogues. The internet is a good place to look for suppliers. Ask for free samples so that you can see and feel the weight and texture of the card – companies should be more than happy to send these out to you. Many card companies offer large discounts when ordering blank cards in large quantities.

Think carefully about your design and order card to complement the look – ivory and cream cards look subtle and stylish when put with gold, but white card looks fresh and clean when combined with lilac and pink (think about cool and warm tones, page 21). A textured card will add interest, and hammered and linen effect cards are also very popular for wedding stationery.

quick & clever Allow yourself plenty of time for the project, from researching suppliers to adding the finishing touches. Work out when the cards will be sent, then assess if you have enough time to complete the job. Cards made with care and attention will look far nicer than those rushed at the last minute.

quick & clever When ordering your cards and envelopes, remember to order some spare in case of mishaps. Doing this in advance saves time, money and ensures the company haven't run out of your chosen card just when you need more!

Don't forget the envelopes: making envelopes is too time consuming but a cheap, office envelope will spoil the overall effect. Order good quality envelopes as these will make your invitations extra special. Luxurious pearl-effect envelopes, or gold and silver foil ones, work well with ivory or cream card.

Finishing touches

Printing inserts on the computer is ideal for ensuring the cards contain all the information you wish to pass on, such as time, date, location and so on. Pick a font that matches the occasion, and paper that tones with your card (see page 15). You may want to leave a blank space to write guests' names by hand afterwards, for a personal touch.

Don't forget to decorate your envelopes, perhaps with just a small version of the design – this adds the finishing touch and co-ordinates the package.

Making up the cards

Enlist the help of family and friends as this will help to spread the load and get the job done quicker. It is also fun to work together, especially when there is a special occasion in the pipeline. Make sure you have ample space in which to work, and keep the area tidy and organised.

Set up the table like a production line – one person does one part of the design; passes it to the next person to do the next bit and then to the last person to stick it on. Do as much as possible in advance, such as punching out shapes, sorting embellishments and ensuring you have enough of each design element, plus some spare.

The Hearts and Flowers Engagement card (see page 74) would also make a lovely wedding invitation.

Selling Your Cards

If you enjoy making cards so much that your production begins to outstrip your needs, then this is a good time to consider selling the extras. You may not make a fortune but you will, at least, cover your costs. There are several outlets, and to follow are some good ideas for packaging and selling your cards.

Where to start

There are many different ways to sell your handmade cards. You can, of course, sell to friends and family and this is how most people get started. If you work in an office, this is another invaluable source of custom. A good way to display your cards for sale to family, friends or work colleagues is in a photo album – the cards won't get touched or damaged. Put together a good selection, but not so many that people are spoiled for choice.
 Try to sell the cards you have and not take orders – it is important to keep the stock moving and not be left with unsold cards for longer than necessary.

Presentation and marketing are the keys to successful selling.

Many people don't have time to spend hours looking in card shops, so they may be happy to buy a couple of cards whilst doing something else – try local gift shops, florists, coffee shops and even hairdressers. Many big department stores also buy direct from crafters so don't be afraid to approach them. Send them a professional looking card sample and covering letter, introducing yourself and what you supply. Card shops tend to buy in bulk – you are more likely to be successful approaching smaller outlets.

Selling to shops

There are two main ways of doing business with shops. Firstly, there is sale or return, which is what the shop is most likely to want. Take a selection of cards into them and agree what you are willing to pay the shop for selling them: a percentage of the cost of each card. Leave them for an allotted time, then return to see what has sold and collect your money – paying the shop their fee – and take back the unsold cards. Keep a list of the cards you leave there, and check off what has been sold so that you know what to make again.

The other way is to take a number of cards into the shop and sell them to the shopkeeper for a set price per card, or for ten or twenty cards. The shop then sells them for whatever they feel they can charge. I prefer to work like this, as you receive the money as you make the cards – and then you can start again.

You probably make slightly more money working on sale and return. However the unsold cards may have been damaged by people looking at them and, of course, you still have to sell them.

Printed labels with your contact details are a great way to encourage business.

Top Tips for Cards That Sell

A rubber stamp is a quick way to add your details to the back of your cards.

Design

Position the design elements towards the top of the card, as this is the part people will see when looking through the rack. Try to offer a selection of cards suitable for everyone and all occasions. Birthday cards are the most frequently bought, so you will need to cater for all ages from little children to teenagers, ladies and men. Floral designs are always popular for women; stick to sporting themes for men, such as golf, football, baseball and fishing to appeal to the widest audience.

Size

The dimensions of your card are very important, and you should try to keep to standard sizing. C6 is the most common size card – this is a folded A5. If you are buying blanks, this will keep the cost down as every card supplier stocks C6 and many of them offer special deals on them. It will also help if you are selling into shops as the standard card rack is made to take this size card – smaller or larger cards may not fit. Visit a few retailers to see how they display their stock.

Matching envelopes really create the professional finish that is so important when selling cards.

Quality

Buy the best card stock you can afford, as cheap card stock will make cheap looking cards. Matching coloured envelopes look fantastic and add the finishing touch, giving a professional look. If you use foil, gold or silver envelopes you will find that you can charge more for your cards, as these definitely look more expensive.

Protective bags will keep your cards clean and are ideal for shop presentation.

Protective bags

Always pack your cards in polypropylene bags (see below left) as this helps to protect them and keep them clean, and this is how they are presented in the shops. Bags are very inexpensive, and are worth the investment as you will present your cards in a much more professional way.

Marketing

If you want to, have labels printed with your contact details to go on the bags so that customers know how to get hold of more of your cards. Stamp the back of your cards so that customers know they are handmade and by whom (see above). Get a rubber stamp made with a little motif and your name, and include your telephone number because if someone receives your card they won't have the bag with your details on.

Pricing

Price your cards individually so that people don't have to ask. Don't under price your cards and make sure you cover the cost of the materials used and add a bit of money for you too. You may not cover your time – but you can enjoy the fruits of a hobby you really enjoy.

Girlie Birthday Card

Simple but stylish – I think this clean, contemporary design makes a great birthday card for girls and women of all ages. A special girlie card!

This is a wonderful card for a beginner to try their hand at, as the techniques are easy and the result is stunning. The funky, silver daisies are mounted on bright aqua-coloured paper vellum and cut out. Wire stems for each of the flowers are neatly trapped under the sheer sticky panel at the bottom of the card. To personalize the greeting, you could add a name or message positioned on top of the panel using rubber stamps or peel off letters.

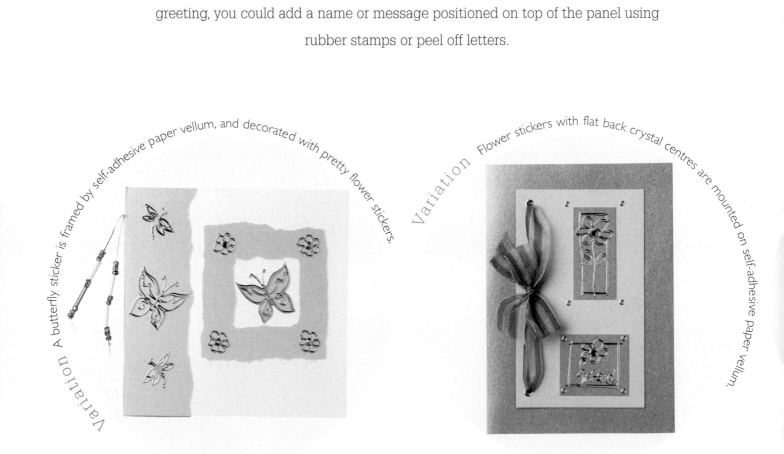

Variation A butterfly sticker is framed by self-adhesive paper vellum, and decorated with pretty flower stickers.

Variation Flower stickers with flat back crystal centres are mounted on self-adhesive paper vellum.

Girlie Birthday Card

You will need

* 12cm (4¾in) folded square white card (see page 11)
* 5.5 x 15cm (2⅛ x 6in) rectangle of soft green self-adhesive paper vellum
* Aqua paper vellum
* Peel off stickers: daisies
* 3 adhesive foam pads
* 22g green wire

Step one
Lift three daisy stickers and position them on the aqua vellum, leaving enough room to cut around each one.

Step two
Cut out each daisy going right up to the edge of the sticker. Try not to leave any of the aqua vellum showing outside the daisy but also be careful not to cut the edge of the sticker.

Step three
Place an adhesive foam pad on the back of each of the vellum daisies.

Step four

Cut three 5cm (2in) lengths of green wire. Remove the backing paper from the foam pads and stick a length of wire to each daisy to make stalks.

Step five

Stick the daisies to the front of the card, positioning the daisy heads towards the top of the card and spacing them evenly across the front of the card.

quick & clever

Do not cut the wire with your scissors, as this will damage them – always use wire cutters.

Step six

Peel back part of the backing paper from the self-adhesive vellum, and line it up with the outside and bottom edge of the card. Peel back the rest of the backing paper and smooth the vellum over the bottom of the card, making sure the wire stems are tucked underneath. The vellum wraps around to the back of the card by about 3cm (1¼in).

quick & clever

If you can't find self-adhesive paper vellum you can use normal paper vellum and stick it to the card using spray adhesive or a Xyron machine.

Kiddie Cat Birthday

Children love bright colours and cute animals, and this card has them both. I have used a rubber stamp, because I can't draw! But for those of you who can, a permanent marker pen can be used to create your own individual designs.

Shrink plastic is a great material. Cut the design out, heat it up and watch it shrink before your very eyes. The motifs bend, twist, curl and finally flatten out to give cute buttons. They shrink to about forty per cent of their original size. Just remember to punch the buttonholes before you heat and shrink them. These cute buttons also look great sewn on a jumper or shirt, or even added to a plain T-shirt.

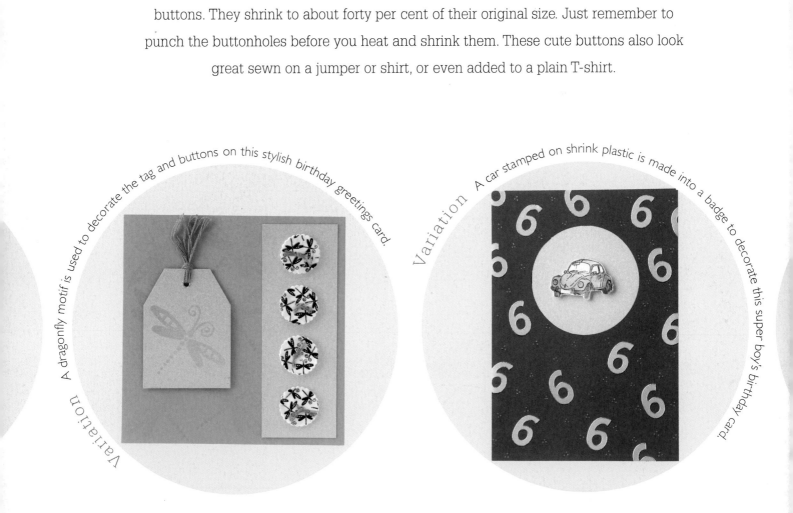

Variation A dragonfly motif is used to decorate the tag and buttons on this stylish birthday greetings card.

Variation A car stamped on shrink plastic is made into a badge to decorate this super boy's birthday card.

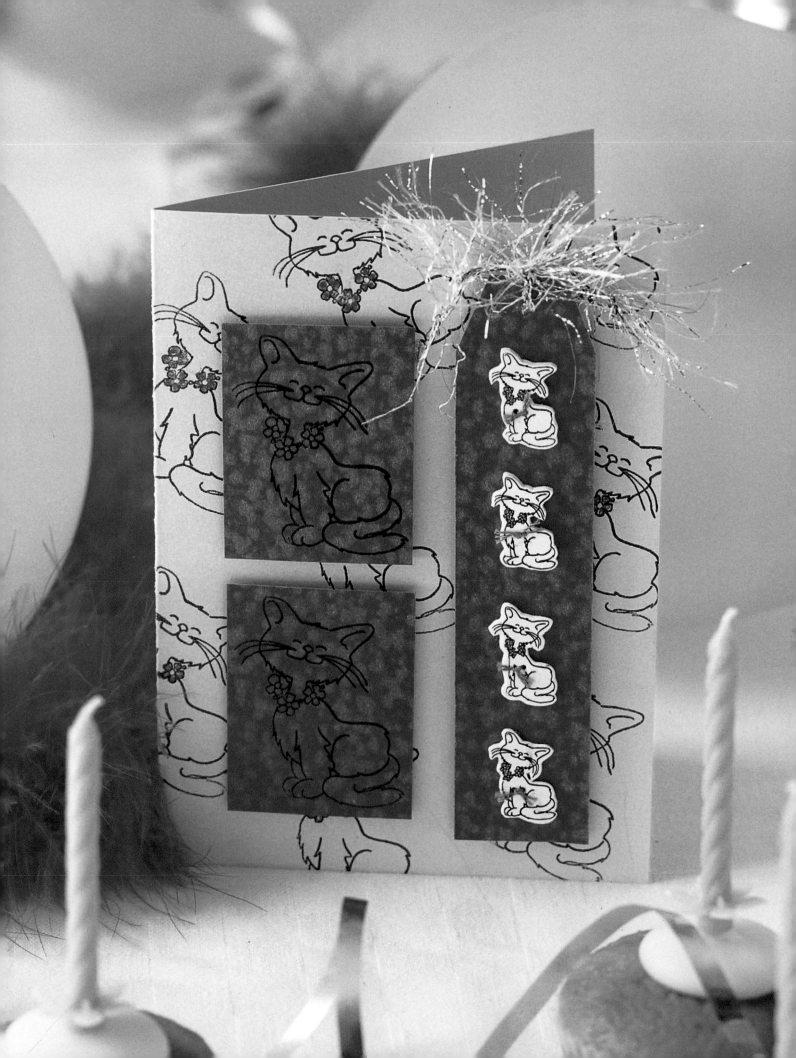

Kiddie Cat Birthday

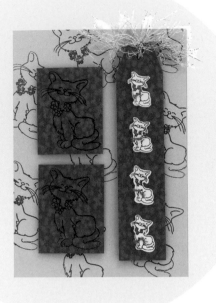

You will need

* A5 pink card, scored and folded to make C6 (see page 14)

* A4 (US letter) bright pink card
* Sheet of shrink plastic
* Sanding block
* Cat rubber stamp
* Black permanent inkpad
* 3mm (⅛in) hole punch
* Heat resistant chopping board
* Heat tool
* Pink embroidery thread
* Pink gel pen
* Adhesive foam pads
* Wispy silver thread

quick & clever ✳ Choose simple, bold designs to make out of shrink plastic. Intricate motifs may tear as you are ✳ cutting them out.

Step one

Sand the sheet of shrink plastic using the sanding block. Rub in all directions to take the glossy finish off. Wipe off the dust. Use the black permanent inkpad to stamp out four cat designs on the shrink plastic leaving plenty of room between them. Leave to dry for a few minutes.

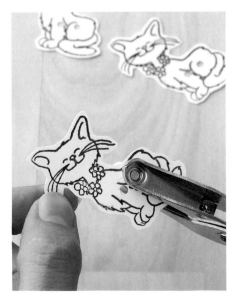

Step two

Cut the cats out of the sheet of shrink plastic, leaving a slight border around them. Use the hole punch to create two holes for the buttons.

Step three

Place one of the cats on the heat resistant chopping board and hold in place with a craft knife. Apply heat with the heat tool. The shrink plastic will twist and curl as it shrinks.

Step four
Keep applying heat to the cat until it finally flattens out. Take the edge of the rubber stamp and press it down on top of the cat to make sure it is nice and flat.

Step five
Cut short lengths of pink embroidery thread. Thread through the buttonholes to the front and tie in a knot. Use the gel pen to colour the flowers around the cats' necks and leave to dry.

Step six
Place your folded pink card on a piece of scrap card and, using the black permanent inkpad and rubber stamp, randomly stamp cats all over the front of your card. Make sure some of the cats spill over the edges to give a professional finish. Leave to dry. Stamp two cat designs on the bright pink card, leaving space between them. Leave to dry then cut around them to make two oblongs. Once dry colour in all the flowers around the cats' necks with the pink gel pen.

Step seven
Trace over the long tag template (see pages 100–102) and apply to the back of the remaining bright pink card. Cut out and stick the cat buttons to the front of the tag with double-sided tape, making sure they are evenly positioned. Position the two oblong cat designs on the left front of the card and stick in place with adhesive foam pads. Punch a hole in the top of the tag and pull the wispy silver thread through the tag. Make a loop at the front and pull the ends through. Stick the tag to the right front of the card using adhesive foam pads.

New Home Celebration

This card was inspired by a paint chart from my local DIY store, and as a new home usually involves some decorating it seemed particularly appropriate. I love to use found elements in my card-making – advertising leaflets are another great source of ideas. Colour co-ordinate your card, inkpad and paint chart for a professional look.

Using paint charts offers an infinite number of colour variations, so experiment with different groups of colour. This card has beautifully muted, toning shades, but why not try bold, contrasting card colours to really catch the eye. The graphic outline of the house works well against the blocks of colour, and who knows – the colours may give the new home owners some interior design ideas!

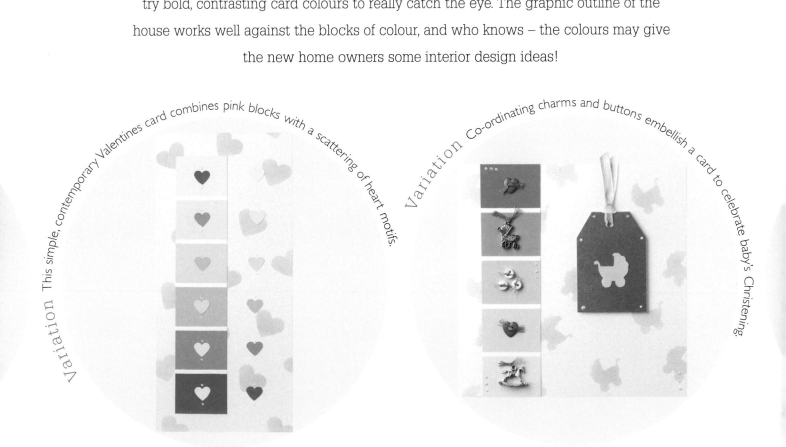

Variation This simple, contemporary Valentines card combines pink blocks with a scattering of heart motifs.

Variation Co-ordinating charms and buttons embellish a card to celebrate baby's Christening.

New Home Celebration

You will need

* A4 (US letter) cream card, scored and folded to A5 (page 14)
* A4 (US letter) fern green card
* A4 (US letter) antique gold card
* Punches: house, key
* Scrap card for stencil
* Pearlized green inkpad
* Cosmetic sponge
* Strip from a paint chart
* Glue pen
* Eyelets, punch and setter tool
* Hammer
* Adhesive foam pads
* String

Step one

Punch a house from the piece of scrap card to make a stencil. Sponge house motifs on to the front of the card using the pearlized green ink and sponge. Position the houses randomly and let them spill over the edges of the card to give a more professional finish.

Step two

Insert the fern green card into the house punch, pushing the paper right to the back of the punch. To make the second house push the card to the back of the punch and line the edge of the punch up with the edge of the first punched out house. Repeat again to give a row of three houses. (Reserve the house motifs for step three.) Allow a border around the house motifs and cut out using a craft knife and metal ruler.

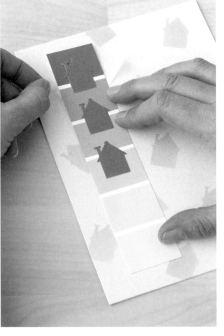

Step three

Cut out six of the colours from the paint chart and stick to the front left of the stencilled card with double-sided tape. Position the three house motifs over the top four squares and tape in place.

Step four

Trace over the tag template (see pages 100–102) and transfer on to the back of the green card. Use a ruler to make sure the lines are straight. Cut out using scissors.

Step five

Punch the key shapes out of antique gold card. Cut around the key shape you want to use with scissors (this particular punch creates three different keys at once), and stick to the tag using a glue pen. Leave to dry for a few minutes.

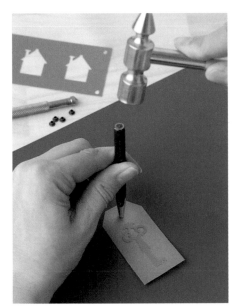

Step six

Position the panel of houses across the bottom of the card, overlapping the paint chart on the left and use the eyelet punch and hammer to make a hole through all layers in each corner of the panel. Add eyelets to each hole. Use the eyelet punch and hammer to create a hole in the tag, and add an eyelet.

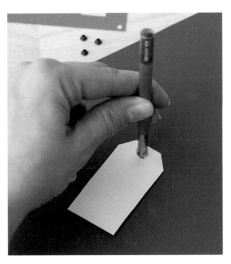

Step seven

Turn the tag and panel of houses and card over and use the setter tool and hammer to flatten the eyelets.

Step eight

Cut a length of string and thread through the tag, making a loop at the front and pulling the ends through. Attach the tag to the top right of the card using foam adhesive pads.

* quick & clever
Cover the eyelet with a piece of spare card and hammer the eyelet flat for a * neat, smooth finish

Spring Flowers Easter Card

For an eye-catching Easter card I used a stencil to create a plaid background, then added a scattering of spring flowers. Orange and yellow are lovely spring colours, just perfect to celebrate the reappearance of the sun after long winter days.

The stencils for the plaid background and daisies are traced from patterns provided in the book then cut out with a craft knife: simplicity itself. Inkpads and a cosmetic sponge provide the colour, and a sprinkling of glitter glue gives the card some super sparkle.

Variation Change the shape of the card and the colours used to create a completely different look – perfect for birthdays.

Variation Create a background using the thin plaid stripe and a stamped motif. Stamp and mount the central flower.

Spring Flowers Easter Card

You will need

* A5 magnolia card, scored and folded to make C6 (see page 14)
* A4 (US letter) magnolia card
* Cosmetic sponges
* Orange and yellow inkpads
* Glitter glue
* Peel off flower eyelets
* Adhesive foam pads

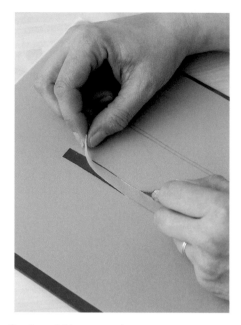

Step one

Trace off the stripes for the plaid pattern (see pages 100–102). Make a tracing paper stencil by cutting the thick and thin stripes out of tracing paper with a craft knife. Rub out any pencil marks. Leave at least 2.5cm (1in) at the top and bottom of the paper as this will stop the ink smudging when sponging.

quick & clever ✳

✳ After you have made the first stripe, place the stencil where you wish to make the second stripe and make a pencil mark on the tracing paper along the edge of the first stripe. Use this mark as a guide for positioning the other stripes evenly.

Step two

Sponge thick vertical lines across the front of the folded card using the tracing paper stencil, cosmetic sponge and orange ink. Move the stencil across the card, leaving an even gap between each stripe, until the card is covered (see Quick & Clever, above right). Leave to dry, then use the thin stencil and a clean sponge to add yellow vertical stripes between the orange stripes, spacing them evenly across the card. Leave to dry.

Step three

Now sponge horizontal stripes over the vertical stripes; first in orange and then in yellow. Leave to dry.

Step four

Trace off the large, medium and small daisy patterns (see pages 100–102) and cut out, using a craft knife, to make stencils. Rub out any remaining pencil marks. Use the tracing paper stencil, cosmetic sponge and orange ink to sponge a large, medium and small daisy on to the A4 (US letter) magnolia card. Then, using a clean sponge and the yellow ink sponge two large daisies and one medium and small daisy. Leave to dry, then cut the daisies out.

Step five

Apply glitter glue to the edges of all the thick orange stripes on the front of the card and set aside to dry.

Step six

Stick a peel off flower eyelet in the centre of each of the daisies and decorate with glitter glue. Leave to dry.

Step seven

Arrange the daisies in a pattern on the front of the card, then use double-sided tape to stick the small and medium daisies in place and adhesive foam pads to attach the large daisies.

Birthday Surprise Pockets

This is a lovely way to send a secret message, poem or love letter to someone; it's particularly appropriate for a surprise birthday celebration. The message is written in a small card hidden in a pocket on the front of a bigger card – so it can stay private even when the card is on display.

The card pockets are made from paper vellum which is sheer but fairly strong, so you can trace the motifs from the back of the book directly on to it. Other lovely ways to create pockets include sewing wide, sheer ribbon to the card using a sewing machine, or using patterned papers that you have bought or created yourself. Write your message on a tag and pop it in the pocket.

Variation A small pocket and a decorative panel are made from patterned paper vellum. A small tag holds the message.

Variation A heart-shaped tag containing a special message is slipped inside a pocket made from decorated paper.

Birthday Surprise Pockets

You will need

* 14.8cm (5¾in) folded square turquoise card (see page 11)
* A4 (US letter) sheet of paper vellum
* A4 (US letter) turquoise card
* A4 (US letter) silver card
* Punches: circle, daisy and square corner cutter
* Paper trimmer
* Daisy sticker
* 3mm (⅛in) hole punch
* Peel off eyelet stickers
* Silver thread
* Seed beads

Step one

Trace the large envelope pocket template (see pages 100–102) straight on to the vellum and cut it out. Score and fold the pattern using a ruler and bone folder to give sharp creases. Create the half circle in the envelope using either a circle punch or cut it out with scissors. Fold in the side edges and attach double-sided tape to them, then bring the bottom section up and stick to the side flaps.

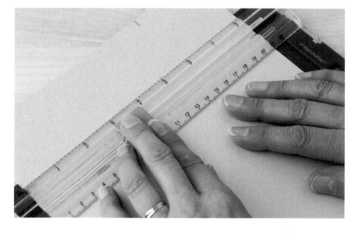

Step two

Use the paper trimmer to cut a rectangle of silver card measuring 15 × 7cm (6 × 2¾in). Score and fold in half to make a small card.

quick & clever ✱
✱ To help keep your punches sharp and in good working order, punch shapes out of kitchen foil or waxed paper from time to time.

Step three

Cut a piece of turquoise card to measure 5.5cm × 6cm (2¼ × 2⅜in). Punch all the corners using the square corner cutter. Centre this punched card on the front of the folded silver card and attach with double-sided tape.

Step four

Cut a 4cm (1⅝in) square of silver card and centre it on the turquoise card with the punched corners and stick in place with double-sided tape. Place the daisy sticker in the middle of the silver card.

Step five

Trace off the small pocket template (see pages 100–102) straight on to the vellum. Fold in the three edges using a bone folder and attach double-sided tape to them (see page 15). Position the pocket in the centre front of the folded turquoise card and stick in place. Pop the small silver card inside.

Step seven

Cut a length of silver thread, long enough to wrap around your large pocket and tie in a bow. Tie a knot in one end and thread some seed beads and a daisy on to the thread, then add another daisy, add some more seed beads and tie a knot at the other end.

Step six

Punch two daisies from turquoise card and use the hole punch to make a hole in one of the petals of each daisy. Stick a peel-off eyelet over the holes on the right side of each daisy.

quick & clever *

* Use patterned paper vellum or a patterned or plain paper to make the large envelope, and the card inside will be hidden until opened.

Step eight

Put the big card into the big pocket and secure with the thread, tying in a bow. Make sure the daisies lie coloured side up.

Découpage Design

Men are so difficult to make cards for, so when I saw a pack of serviettes with garden motifs decorating them, I immediately thought of my dad and the many men like him, who are avid gardeners.

Scour the shops for all sorts of serviette decorations. Christmas serviettes are ideal for Christmas cards. Separate out the patterned layer of the serviette and glue it to card before cutting out. The images on the serviette used for this project were contained in tag shapes, but you could always draw your own tag shapes around motifs before cutting them out. Adding eyelets and string finishes the rustic look.

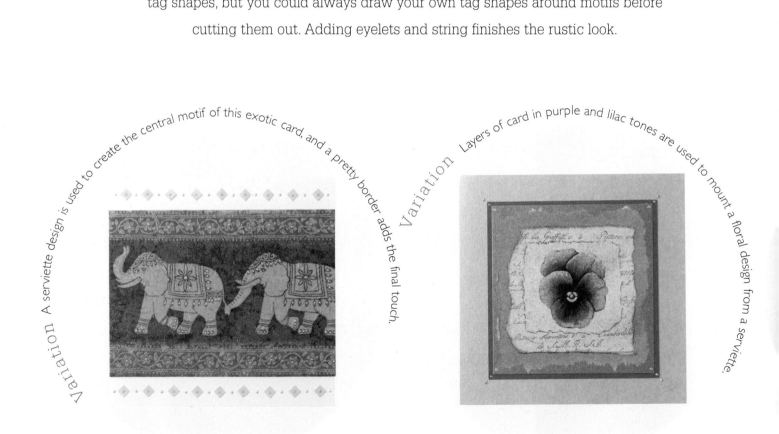

Variation A serviette design is used to create the central motif of this exotic card, and a pretty border adds the final touch.

Variation Layers of card in purple and lilac tones are used to mount a floral design from a serviette.

Découpage Design

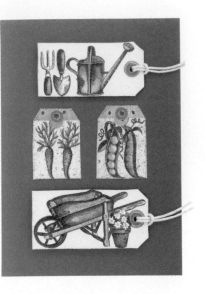

* A5 fern green card, scored and folded to make C6 (see page 14)
* A4 (US letter) white card
* Patterned serviettes
* Spray adhesive
* Box to spray into
* 3mm (⅛in) hole punch
* Peel off sticker eyelets
* String
* Adhesive foam pads

Step one

Separate out the top layer of serviette that has the pattern on. Rub your thumbnail over the embossed dots around the edge of the serviette to flatten them, this will make it easier to separate the layers

quick & clever *

* When using spray adhesive, work in a well-ventilated room or outside, and read the instructions before starting. You may want to use a face-mask for extra protection.

Step two

Place the patterned layer of serviette in the cardboard box, pattern side down. Hold the spray adhesive a few centimetres away from the serviette, and apply a fine layer of glue.

Step three

Stick the serviette to the A4 (US letter) white card and use your fingers to smooth the serviette in place. You can carefully peel back the serviette if you get wrinkles and smooth it down again.

Step four

Cut out four images with scissors. You will need two long horizontal images and two small vertical images to create this design.

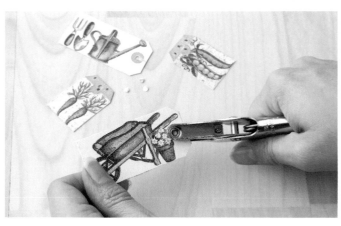

Step five

Using the hole punch, make a hole in the ends of each of the picture tags.

Step six

Use a craft knife to peel off a sticker eyelet and carefully position this over the hole in one of the picture tags. Repeat with the other tags.

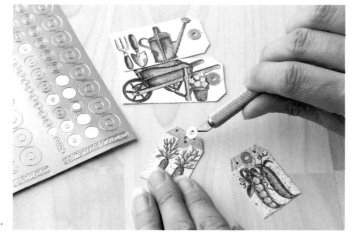

Step seven

Cut two short lengths of string. Fold one in half and thread it through one of the longer tags, thread the string ends through the loop and pull tight. Repeat with the second long tag.

Step eight

Attach one of the longer images to the bottom front of the card using adhesive foam pads. Stick the two smaller images next to each other above it, using double-sided tape. Position the final image at the top of the card, and secure with adhesive foam pads.

Woven Wedding Anniversary

Hearts symbolize love and romance, which is just what is needed for an anniversary card. I have recently celebrated my 20th wedding anniversary, which is represented by paper, so this woven heart – to express my love – was quite simply perfect.

You can buy pre-cut strips of paper or card or you can cut your own. This heart uses colours that fall close together on the colour wheel: pinks and mauves in a variety of tones. Similar colours create a harmonious effect; contrasting colours such as red and green that are opposite each other on the colour wheel produce a big, bold design. You can cut any shape you want from the woven strips, as long as you apply wide double-sided tape to the back first, as this holds all the strips together.

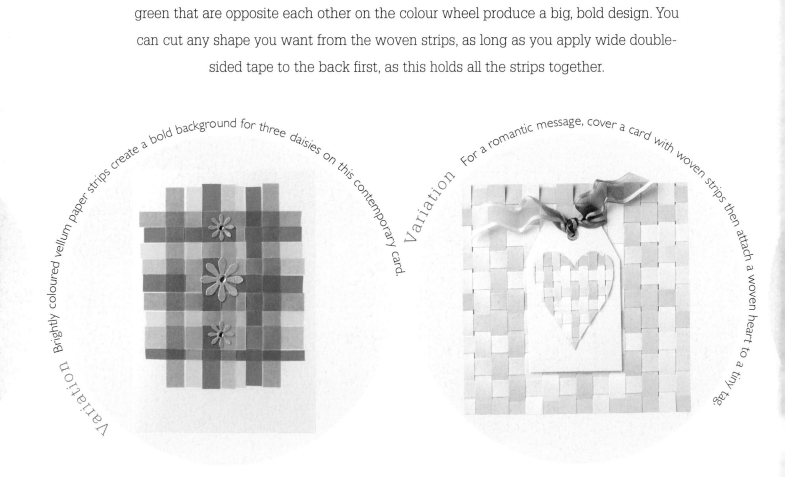

Variation Brightly coloured vellum paper strips create a bold background for three daisies on this contemporary card.

Variation For a romantic message, cover a card with woven strips then attach a woven heart to a tiny tag.

50

Woven Wedding Anniversary

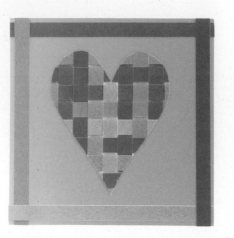

You will need

* 14.8cm (5¾in) folded square silver card (see page 11)
* twenty to twenty-five strips of coloured card, each 1 x 29.5cm (⅜ x 11⅝in)
* Normal and wide double-sided tape
* Glue pen

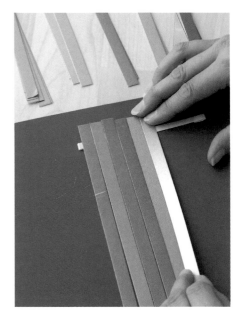

Step one

Trace over the heart template (see pages 100–102). Cut a strip of normal width double-sided tape slightly longer than the width of the heart pattern. Place it across the top of a craft mat and remove the top backing paper so it is sticky side up. Secure the ends by turning them over and sticking them to the craft mat. Stick the strips of coloured card on to the tape, leaving a slight overhang at the top and making sure the strips line up evenly. You will need approximately ten strips.

Step two

Start to weave across, taking the first strip of card under then over the next strip until you reach the other end. The next strip will go over then under the vertical strips. Keep alternating until you have ten horizontal strips.

Step three

Carefully pull the tape holding the woven strips from the cutting mat, and turn the woven square over. Stick two strips of wide, double-sided tape to the back of the woven strips and this will help to hold all the pieces together.

Step four

Transfer the heart pattern to a piece of plain paper, cut around and place it on the right side of the woven strips. Draw around it carefully.

Step five

Cut the heart shape out of the woven card strips. If any of the woven strips look loose on the front of the heart, use a glue pen to stick them to the card strip underneath.

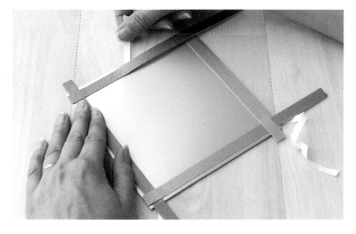

Step six

Apply double-sided tape to the back of four more strips of coloured paper (see page 15). Position one down each edge of the front of the silver card and stick in place.

Step seven

Open the card out and trim off the overhanging strips of paper.

quick & clever *

*   Always keep patterns such as the heart. Label them and file them away, ready to be used the next time you make this card – or create an alternative design.

Step eight

Position the woven heart centrally inside the border using a set square to guide you, and peel back the backing paper from the wide double-sided tape.

Father's Day Metallic Card

Every father deserves a unique card to celebrate his special day and this Celtic design is ideal. I had a blank triangle card I had bought previously and the two went together perfectly. I am sure any man would be fascinated by this metal card and would love to see how it is made. Watch out though, you might find your equipment disappearing!

The metal design is made from pure copper and amazing things happen when it is heated. It changes in colour from bright copper, to tarnished copper to pink, then purple and finally to a bluey silver and gold. Do remember that only pure copper metal will change colour – there are coated copper-coloured metal sheets available, but these will not give the desired effect.

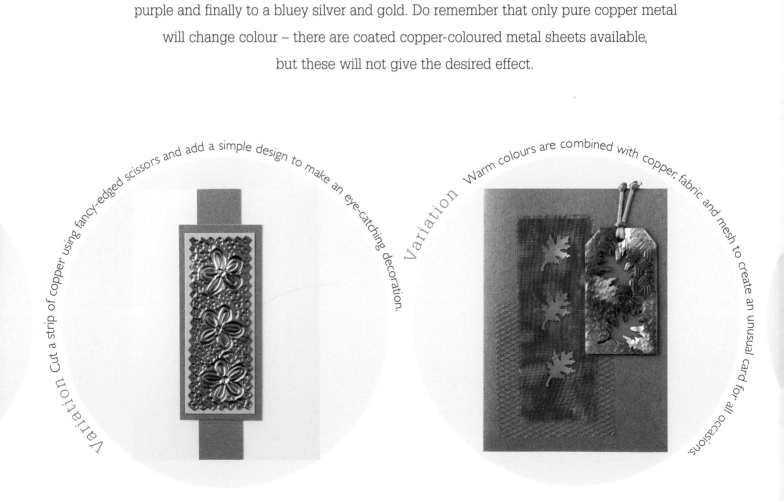

Variation Cut a strip of copper using fancy-edged scissors and add a simple design to make an eye-catching decoration.

Variation Warm colours are combined with copper, fabric and mesh to create an unusual card for all occasions.

Father's Day Metallic Card

You will need

* 16 x 16 x 16cm (6¼ x 6¼ x 6¼in) bought blank triangle card
* Foam sheet
* Pure copper metal sheet
* Embossing tool
* Heat resistant chopping board
* Heat tool
* Guillotine or scissors
* Adhesive foam pads

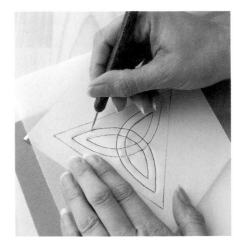

Step one
Using tracing paper and pencil trace over the Celtic design template (see page 100–102). Lay the copper sheet on top of the foam sheet, place the tracing paper design on top and using the embossing tool carefully trace over the pencil lines of the design. You need to apply about the same pressure as you would for writing. As you work, lift up the tracing paper occasionally to see if the pattern is clear.

* quick & clever*

Rub the end of an embossing tool in candle wax and it will glide over tracing paper and avoid tearing it when you are transferring an image. Keep reapplying the wax as you work.

Step two
Working on the heat resistant board, heat the copper sheet with the heat tool. The copper will change colour from bright copper to a tarnished orange. The copper changes colour exactly at the spot where the heat is directed.

Step three
Keep heating the copper sheet and it will change to a pinky colour and then to purple.

Step four

Finally the copper changes to a bluey silver and gold. Leave the copper until it is cold.

Step five

Place the copper sheet on the foam again and use a ruler and the embossing tool to draw a triangle around the design. Draw the line about 1.25cm (½in) from the design.

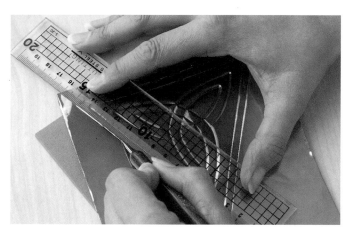

Step six

Using the embossing tool draw a second triangle about 6mm (¼in) outside the first triangle.

Step seven

Continue working with the copper on the foam sheet and use the embossing tool with a stabbing motion to create a hammered effect on the metal. Don't go too close to the design or you will flatten out the edges and lose the pattern.

Step eight

Use the guillotine or scissors to cut out the design, cutting just outside the second triangle outline. Stick the triangular Celtic design to the front of the triangle card using adhesive foam pads.

Glittering Mosaic Thank You

Show your appreciation in style with this sparkling thank you card. Here, I show you how to create a beautiful mosaic panel, decorated with ultra fine glitter to give a very subtle sparkle to the card. The matching tag makes an effective embellishment and, if you were feeling generous, could easily adorn a present.

The mosaic punch is so versatile – use it once for the fabulous gift tag, and create a stunning repeat-pattern panel by using it several times. The design is very intricate and so is best used with paper to get crisp, clean cuts. Choose copper, gold and green papers and cards for the men in your life. Pinks, purples and lilacs are a wonderful combination for a ladies card.

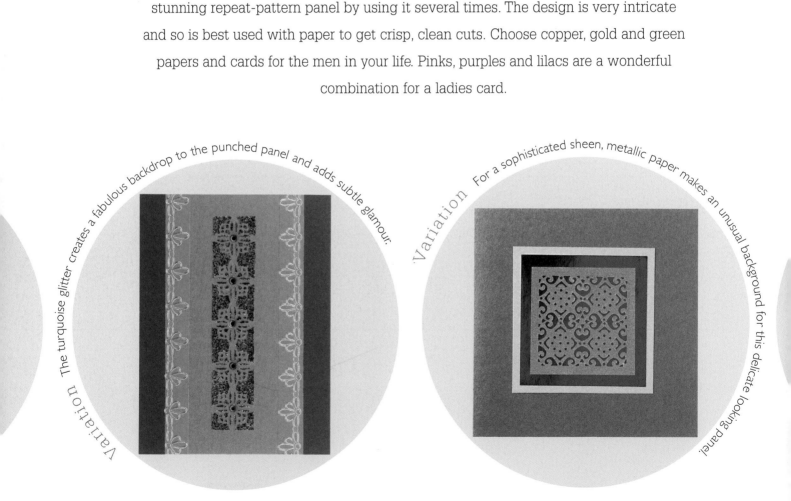

Variation The turquoise glitter creates a fabulous backdrop to the punched panel and adds subtle glamour.

Variation For a sophisticated sheen, metallic paper makes an unusual background for this delicate looking panel.

Glittering Mosaic Thank You

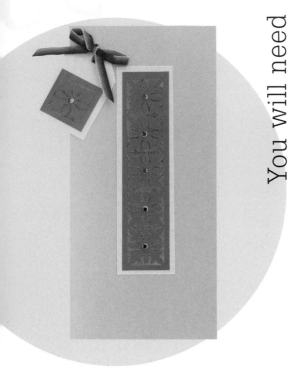

You will need

* 20cm (7⅞in) square silver card, scored and folded to make 10 x 20cm (4 x 7⅞in)
* A4 (US letter) soft pink card
* A4 (US letter) raspberry paper
* Mosaic punch
* A4 (US letter) double-sided adhesive paper
* Ultra fine glitter in pink and purple
* Paper trimmer
* 3mm (⅛in) hole punch
* Peel off eyelet stickers in silver
* Pink ribbon
* Flat back crystals
* Oyster-coloured dimensional glue

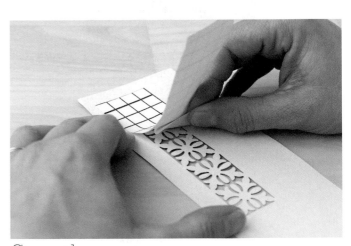

Step one

Cut a strip of raspberry paper at least 8cm (3in) wide and insert it into the mosaic punch, pushing the paper right into the back of the punch and lining up the edge of the punch with the edge of the paper.

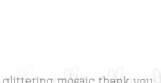

Step two

To make the second mosaic motif turn the punch upside down, push the raspberry paper to the back of the punch and line up the first mosaic with the edge of the design on the punch. Repeat this five times so you have a long strip of punched out motifs.

Step three

Cut a 4 x 13.5cm (1½ x 5¼in) rectangle from the double-sided adhesive paper. Turn the paper with the mosaic design to the wrong side. Partially remove one side of the backing from the adhesive paper. Line up over punched design and stick down.

Step four

Turn the raspberry paper to the right side. Sprinkle glitter over the design and rub in gently with your fingertips. Tip and gently brush off any excess glitter and put it back in the pot.

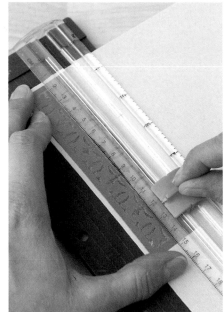

Step five

Using a craft knife or a paper trimmer, cut out the mosaic panel leaving a small border around the edge. Mount this on to the soft pink card using double-sided tape. Trim the pink card to leave a small border around the mosaic panel. Centre the mosaic panel on the front of the silver card and stick in place using double-sided tape (see page 15).

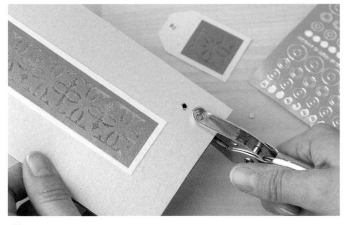

Step six

Trace around the tag template (see pages 100–102), transfer to the back of the soft pink card and cut out. Punch a mosaic square out of raspberry paper, back with double-sided adhesive paper and add glitter as before. Stick this motif to the pink tag. Use the hole punch to make a hole in the tag and add a peel off eyelet sticker. Make two holes in the top left hand corner of the card and add eyelet stickers.

Step seven

Thread the ribbon through the holes on the card and the tag and secure with a bow.

Step eight

Apply a dot of dimensional glue to the centre of each of the mosaic motifs and add a flat back crystal. Leave to dry for about 15 minutes.

quick & clever

The easiest way to position the crystals is to have them face up and pick them up on the end of a licked finger. You can also lick the end of a piece of dry spaghetti and the crystal will stick to it.

Congratulations On Your Baby

Here's a special way to welcome a new baby. Colourful pink baby-grows hang on a washing line and cute little animal buttons add extra decoration to the front of this jolly congratulations card. The beautiful bright colours make it really stand out from the usual soft pastels used for baby arrivals.

This card uses a combination of techniques. A serviette pattern is used to make the background for the front of the card and a rubber stamp provides a simple template for the baby-grows. The miniature pegs can be found in craft shops, stationers and even large supermarkets in a variety of colours.

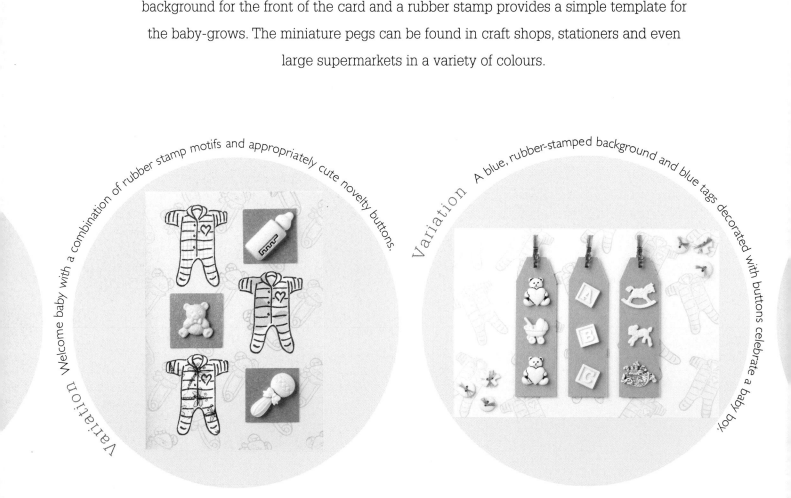

Variation Welcome baby with a combination of rubber stamp motifs and appropriately cute novelty buttons.

Variation A blue, rubber-stamped background and blue tags decorated with buttons celebrate a baby boy.

Congratulations On Your Baby

You will need

* 14.8cm (5¾in) folded square beige card (see page 11)
* Serviette with grass and sky pattern
* Decorative pink paper
* Pink card
* Adhesive spray
* Black permanent inkpad
* Baby-grow rubber stamp
* Kebab sticks
* String
* All purpose sticky craft glue
* Four miniature pink pegs
* Two animal design buttons

Step one

Separate out the patterned layer of serviette. Rub your thumbnail over the embossed dots around the edge of the serviette to flatten them, this will make it easier to separate the layers. Open out the folded beige card and place it on the serviette. Cut around it roughly.

Step two

Place the opened card inside the box, with the right side of the card facing up, and spray with adhesive. Hold the serviette taught over your card, then smooth it down using your fingers to get all the creases out. Rub over any embossed dots to flatten them. Cut the excess serviette from around the card.

Step three

Using the black inkpad stamp out three baby grow designs with the rubber stamp: two on the decorative pink paper and one on the pink card. Leave to dry and then cut around the shapes.

Step four

Cut two kebab sticks roughly 10cm (4in) long. Work on a cutting mat with a craft knife or use scissors, if preferred.

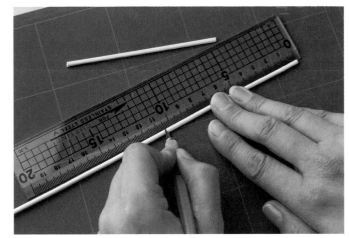

quick & clever ✷

✷ Congratulation cards for multiple births can be hard to find – here is the solution. Use two or more baby-grows and choose appropriate colours for the sexes of the babies.

Step five

Lay the kebab sticks on the front of the card to make two ends of a washing line, and cut a piece of string slightly longer than needed to go between the two. Tie the string in a knot around one of the sticks and make a loose knot around the other. Pull the string tight then trim to the required length.

Step six

Apply all-purpose sticky craft glue to the back of the kebab sticks with another kebab stick then stick in place on the card and leave to dry for 15–20 minutes. Do not worry if you can see some of the excess glue, as it will dry clear. Peg the clothes to the washing line.

Step seven

Using sticky craft glue mount one animal design button at the bottom of a pole and the other beside it on the grass.

Floral Get Well

This card is sure to raise the spirits of anyone who is not well. Pretty flowers in soft, subtle tones are used to decorate the front of two little windows, which each open to reveal a single bloom inside. I've used watercolour pencils to add colour, or you could try felt-tip pens for a bolder finished effect.

A double flower rubber stamp makes it easy to create the windows for this project, as the panel outline provides a guide for cutting around. The window technique can be used with all sorts of cards: hide a motif of something close to the heart of the recipient inside the window or even add a special message!

Variation A single aperture card using the same floral window design in pink, creates a special birthday card.

Variation A simple rubber stamp leaf motif, softly coloured with watercolour pencils, makes a great card for a man.

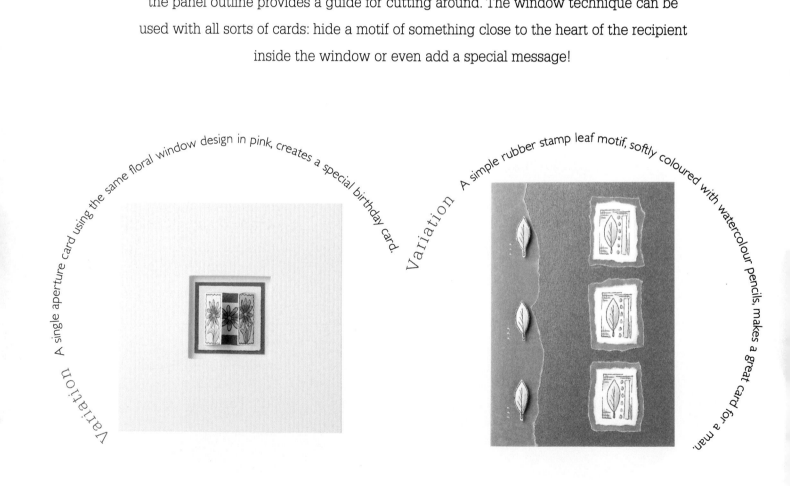

Floral Get Well

You will need

* 12cm (4¾in) folded square cream card (see page 11)
* A4 (US letter) cream card
* A4 (US letter) gold card
* Rubber stamps: double flower, single flower bloom
* Black permanent inkpad
* Watercolour pencils in yellow, orange and green
* Very fine paint brush
* Embossing tool
* Small square punch
* Soft gold dimensional glue

Step one

Using the black inkpad, stamp the double flower design on to the A4 (US letter) cream card, leaving space for a narrow border around the edge of the design. Repeat. Then stamp two of the single flower blooms.

Step two

Colour in the flowers using watercolour pencils. Wet the paintbrush and carefully go over the colours, this will give a more painterly effect. You can add tone by adding more colour in certain areas if you like. Leave to dry.

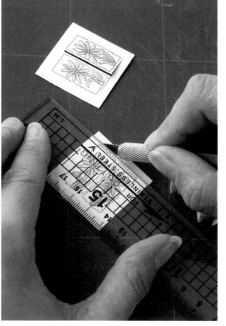

Step three

Using a craft knife and metal ruler cut out each of the double flower designs leaving a narrow border around the edges. Use the panel outlines as a guide and cut down the centre of each design from top to bottom, then across the top and bottom to make windows that open.

Step four

Use an embossing tool and a metal-edged ruler to score the outside edges of each window, this gives a professional finish when you fold them back.

quick & clever ✳

Increase the size of the window then add a special message inside. Use rubber stamps, peel off stickers or write the message by hand.

Step five

Use the small square punch upside down, so that you can see where you will be punching. Place over the top of the single bloom and punch out, repeat with the other single bloom.

Step six

Cut two 4.5cm (1¾in) squares from the gold card. Centre each window on a gold square and stick in place using double-sided tape (see page 15).

Step seven

Stick your mounted windows to the main card. Use a set square to position them evenly, leaving the same border on the right and left hand side. Stick a single bloom inside each window using double-sided tape, then add a dab of soft gold dimensional glue to the centre of each flower to decorate.

21ST Birthday
Congratulations

A twenty-first birthday is a landmark occasion and deserves a special card to celebrate. This is one of my favourite card designs – it is so quick and easy to make but looks sensational. The number twenty-one and the keys spell out the occasion: I created the keys from punches and the card has been decorated with sponged keys as well. The metallic thread and beads make it look like you spent a fortune in a card shop.

Bought stickers have been used as an extra embellishment for this project. Stickers come in all shapes, sizes and designs and are a fun way to make a card in minutes that looks like you have taken hours over it! A daisy chain design on clear card gives a contemporary feel to this card.

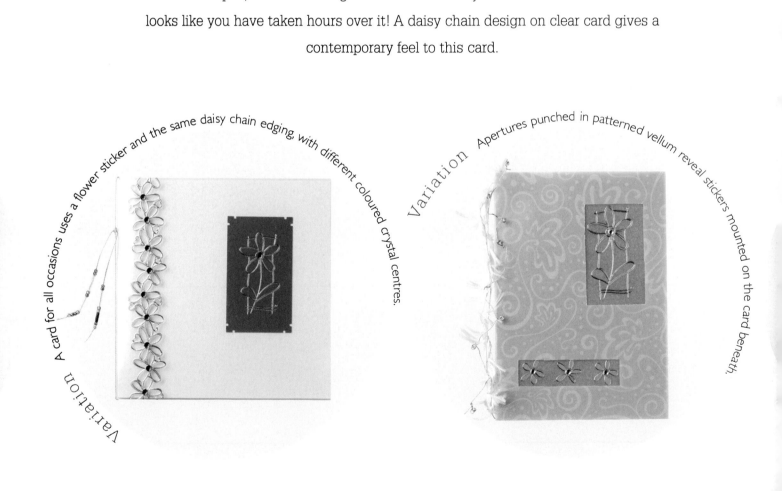

Variation A card for all occasions uses a flower sticker and the same daisy chain edging, with different coloured crystal centres.

Variation Apertures punched in patterned vellum reveal stickers mounted on the card beneath.

21ST Birthday Congratulations

You will need

* ✽ 14.8cm (5¾in) folded square card, white with gold sparkle (see page 11)
* ✽ A4 (US letter) soft green card
* ✽ A4 (US letter) gold card
* ✽ 14.8cm (5¾in) folded bought square clear card
* ✽ Paper trimmer
* ✽ Square corner cutter punch
* ✽ Keys punch
* ✽ 3mm (⅛in) hole punch
* ✽ Peel off eyelet, numbers and daisy chain stickers
* ✽ Gold metallic thread
* ✽ Seed and bugle beads
* ✽ Pale green inkpad
* ✽ Cosmetic sponge
* ✽ Flat back crystals
* ✽ Dimensional glue

quick & clever ✽

✽ You really need to buy mechanically scored and folded clear card. Most acetate is too thick to be folded into a professional-looking card.

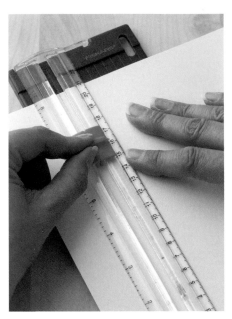

Step one
Cut a 4.5 × 8cm (1¾ × 3⅛in) strip of soft green card using a paper trimmer.

Step two
Punch the corners of the green strip using the square corner cutter.

Step three
Punch keys from the gold card, then cut around the keys you want to use. Use the hole punch to make two holes, one above the other, in the centre top of the strip of green card. Add peel off sticker eyelets. Take a length of gold metallic thread and tie several knots at one end. Thread half a dozen seed beads on and tie several knots at the other end. Slide half the beads down to the other end. Take the thread through the holes on the green card and the punched out keys, and tie in a bow.

Step four

Take the numbers two and one from the sticker sheet, and position under the keys on the green card. Use a craft knife to help you place them accurately.

Step five

Punch out and cut around another key. Using the cosmetic sponge and pale green inkpad, gently sponge around the key on the front of the white card with gold sparkle. Position the key motifs randomly all over the front, making sure they tip over the edge of the card to give a more professional finish.

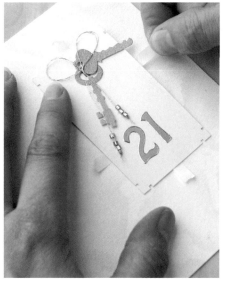

Step six

Position the strip of green card centrally and slightly towards the top of the folded card. Stick in place with double-sided tape (see page 15).

Step seven

Position the daisy chain peel off sticker down the folded edge on the front of the folded clear card. Trim off any excess with scissors. Add flat back crystals to the centres of all the daisies using dimensional glue. If wished, cut out one peel off daisy and stick it to the back of the folded white and gold card, and print or rubber stamp your name underneath so that the person you are sending the card to knows it is handmade.

Step eight

Cut a length of metallic thread that is approximately three times the length of your card. Thread the bugle and seed beads on to the thread, and tie knots at both ends. Place the white and gold card inside the clear card and use the thread to tie the two cards together at the fold. Allow the knot to fall about a third of the way down the outside of the card.

Hearts and Flowers Engagement

A handmade engagement card is the perfect way to congratulate a happy couple. Gold, metal hearts and gold flowers symbolize love and a sprinkling of tiny glass beads give a luxurious finish to this stunning card. I used a blank, nine square aperture card and placed my decorations inside each of the little windows. Although it is possible to cut your own apertures, you will never achieve the professional look of a bought blank card. When you need multiple apertures I think it is always worth spending the money on a bought blank.

Some of the aperture squares are covered with clear sticky squares that the embellishments are added to, and sometimes the decoration is stuck to the inside of the card so it can be seen through the little windows.

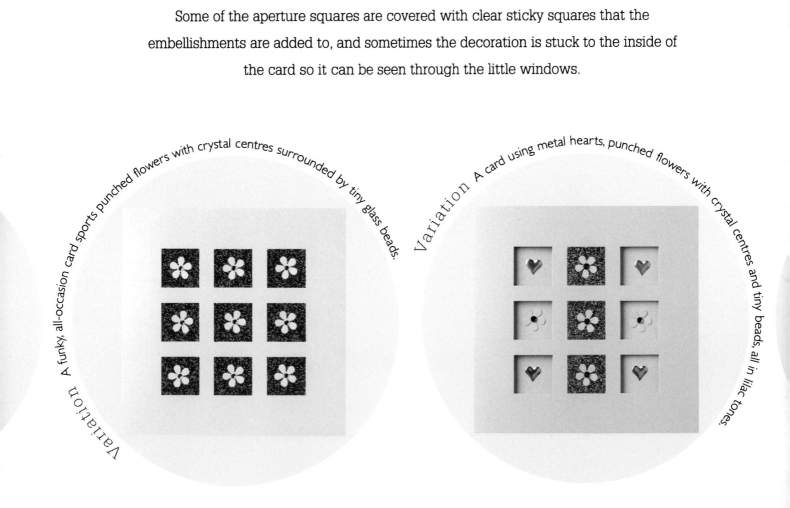

Variation A funky, all-occasion card sports punched flowers with crystal centres surrounded by tiny glass beads.

Variation A card using metal hearts, punched flowers with crystal centres and tiny beads, all in lilac tones.

Hearts and Flowers Engagement

You will need

* 14.8cm (5¾in) folded square coral blank card with nine apertures
* Envelope
* Peel off stickers: clear sticky squares, daisy stickers
* 5 gold, metal hearts
* Tiny no hole glass beads, coral mix
* Self-seal bag
* Dimensional glue
* Flower power punch
* A4 (US letter) double-sided adhesive paper

Step one

Working on a plastic surface and from the inside of your card, place a clear sticky square over the middle square on your card. Place other peel off stickers on the squares above, below and to each side of the centre square to form a cross shape.

Step two

Turn the card over and position a gold, metal heart in the middle of the centre square and firm it down really well, so that the beads cannot get underneath it. Position a daisy sticker in the centre of each of the surrounding four squares and firm down well.

Step three

Place the tiny no hole glass beads into the self-seal bag. Push your card into the bag and use your fingers to rub the beads over the top of the sticky squares.

Step four

Close the card and apply a dot of dimensional glue to the centre of each of the remaining squares, on the inside of the card.

Step five

Lick your finger so that you can pick up the gold metal hearts and stick one in the centre of each of the squares. Leave to dry.

Step six

To decorate the envelope, punch out three flowers from double-sided adhesive paper using the flower power punch.

Step seven

Peel off one side of the backing paper and position the flowers down the left-hand side of the envelope. Remember to leave plenty of room for the address. Remove the top backing paper.

Step eight

Place the envelope in the bag of tiny no hole glass beads, and rub the beads over the daisy shapes. Shake off any excess beads and remove the envelope.

Keepsake Birthday Card

A birthday celebration is the most common reason for sending a card. This is a lovely idea for Granny or Grandpa who will always be pleased to see pictures of their grandchildren. It's popular with aunties, uncles and godparents as well!

Cut down a strip of negatives to make an unusual border to set the images off – but make sure you use negatives that you do not need anymore. This idea can be applied to all sorts of situations, it makes a fun reminder of a holiday with a friend or a memento of a favourite pet.

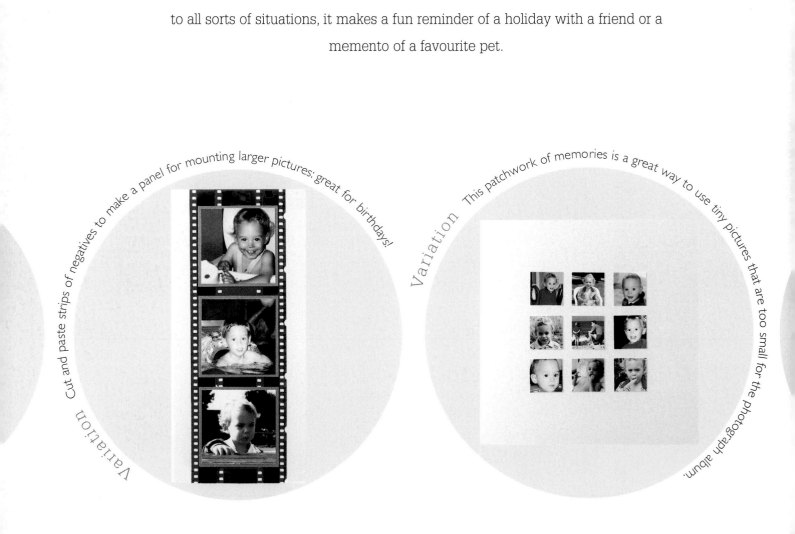

Variation Cut and paste strips of negatives to make a panel for mounting larger pictures: great for birthdays!

Variation This patchwork of memories is a great way to use tiny pictures that are too small for the photograph album.

Keepsake Birthday Card

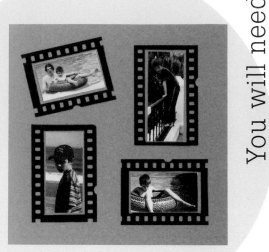

You will need

* 12cm (4¾in) folded square turquoise card (see page 11)
* Photographs
* Negatives
* Super Glue

quick & clever

You can save your original photographs by using colour photocopies, or scanning the pictures into your computer and printing them out.

Step one

Using a craft knife and metal-edged ruler cut out the pictures from a strip of negatives to create several window borders.

Step two

Use the windows to help you select details from larger photographs that will work within the frames. Make sure the image fits the window, mark around the inside of the negative border with a pencil and cut out the photograph using a craft knife and metal ruler.

Step three

For images that are slightly longer or shorter than your negative windows, cut out a small window from a negative strip, then place the strip over the photographic image and cut through both to make a border that fits the image.

quick & clever

To mount small pictures that are all the same size, a square punch, used upside down, is an easy way to select images.

Step four

Apply double-sided tape to the back of cut down photographs (see page 15). Position the photographs on the front of the card, moving them around until you have created a design you like and remembering that the negative borders will take up extra space. Stick down.

Step five

Carefully apply Super Glue to the reverse side of the negatives, taking care that it does not seep through the holes along each side to the front of the plastic strips.

quick & clever

If you are worried about glueing your fingers together, use a pair of tweezers to hold the negatives as you work.

Step six

Stick the negative borders around the photographs on the front of the card.

quick & clever

Adapt this card to mark an 18th or 21st birthday. Select baby, toddler, school and more recent photographs and create a photomontage to mark the occasion.

Mother's Day Posy

Receiving flowers is always special and this pretty, pressed flower Mother's Day card will last a lot longer than fresh ones! I have used bought dried flowers which are ideal for craft projects, but you could make the card extra special by pressing flowers from your own or your mum's garden. Dimensional glue has a raised texture when dry and comes in all different colours, so I've used it in the same way as a highlighter pen on this card, and you can use the same technique on other cards.

Encasing the flowers between sticky, clear plastic helps to preserve and protect them. You can use the same technique to preserve other delicate objects such as feathers, dried grasses or colourful autumn leaves.

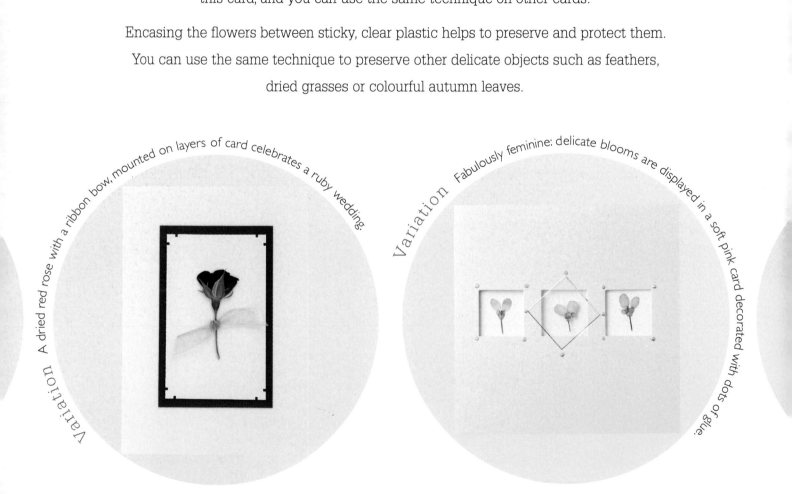

Variation A dried red rose with a ribbon bow, mounted on layers of card celebrates a ruby wedding.

Variation Fabulously feminine: delicate blooms are displayed in a soft pink card decorated with dots of glue.

82

Mother's Day Posy

You will need

＊ 12cm (4¾in) folded square mauve blank card with three apertures

＊ Peel off stickers: clear sticky squares

＊ Pressed flowers

＊ Glue pen

＊ Dimensional glue

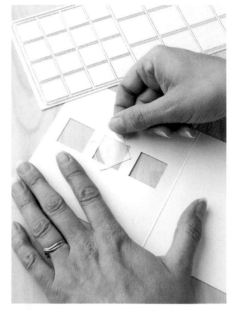

Step one

Open your card so that you are working on the inside of your card, and place one of the sticky squares over the middle aperture. Position it at an angle, like a diamond. Make sure you are working on a plastic surface, as the sticker may stick to the work surface.

Step two

Turn the card over to the front and place one of the pressed flowers on top of the sticky square.

Step three

Take another sticky square and place it directly over the top of the other square, matching the angle. Firm around the edges so the flower is held securely between the two stickers.

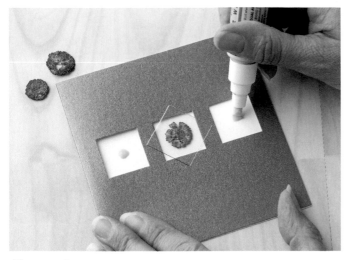

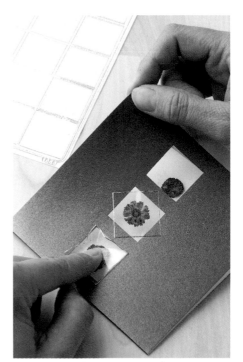

quick & clever

Use an embossing tool to firm around the edge of the flower and ensure the sticky square is firmly positioned on the square.

Step four

Close the card and, using the glue pen, put a dab of glue in the middle of the two outside apertures. The glue comes out blue but dries clear. Position two flowers on the glue and apply pressure until they are stuck in place.

Step five

Continue with the card shut and position a sticky square through one of the outside apertures and over a flower. Working through the aperture will help you position the sticker correctly. Carefully open the card and firm the edges of the sticker down. Repeat through the other aperture.

Step six

Apply a dot of dimensional glue to each corner of the outside apertures and to each point of the sticker diamond on the centre aperture. Squeeze the glue very gently. Leave to dry.

quick & clever

You can easily buy blank cards with apertures – and they look much more professional than hand-cut cards. Apertures come in all shapes and sizes so you can buy a card to match the object you wish to display.

Concertina Christening Card

A baby's christening is a very special occasion and here's a delightful card, which the proud parents are sure to want to keep and treasure. I'm a big fan of stickers and often use them as part of my card creations. For this project I've used a daisy sticker in an unusual way; to create a stencilled background for the main card.

Rubber stamps, beads, buttons and ribbon are just some of the other elements used to create this special keepsake which looks a million dollars but is easy to assemble. A photograph of the baby being christened is hidden inside the concertina card and will give the parents a lovely surprise.

Variation For an exotic feel, use stickers to decorate the card and concertina tag and a wide, fancy ribbon tied in a bow.

Variation Mirror card decorated with gold stickers and finished with a bold ribbon creates a luxurious greetings card.

Concertina Christening Card

You will need

* A5 pink card, scored and folded to make C6 (see page 14)
* A4 (US letter) pink card
* Baby photograph
* Peel off stickers: daisy, clear sticky squares and daisy panel
* Brilliance pink inkpad
* Cosmetic sponge
* Embossing tool
* Floral pattern rubber stamp
* Daisy punch
* Tiny, no hole pink glass beads and self-seal plastic bag
* Flat back crystals
* Dimensional glue
* Heart and teddy bear buttons
* Pink embroidery thread
* 40cm (16in) pink ribbon

Step one

Place a daisy sticker anywhere on the front of the folded pink card. Use the cosmetic sponge to carefully apply ink from the inkpad around the daisy. Lift the sticker and move to another part of the card and repeat. Sponge daisy motifs randomly across the front of the card – make sure to tip the daisies over the edges for a professional finish.

Step two

Cut a 6.5 x 30cm (2⅝ x 11¾in) rectangle from the remaining pink card. Use the embossing tool and ruler to score at 5cm (2in) intervals across the length of the strip, then fold into a concertina booklet. Open it out and work on the last panel on the right. Cut a frame from the centre of the panel, slightly smaller than the photograph you are using. Use the rubber stamp and pink inkpad to print around the edge of the panel.

Step three

On the front of the booklet – the first panel on the left – use the same rubber stamp and pink ink and print one motif in the centre of the panel.

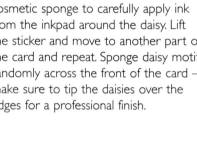

Step four

On the second panel, slide a daisy punch down from the top and punch out the shape. Turn the strip over and stick a clear sticky square over the daisy.

Step five

Put the tiny pink glass beads into the self-seal plastic bag. Slide in the concertina strip and use your fingers to firm the beads on to the sticky daisy. Shake the excess beads back into the bag.

Step six

Stencil a daisy pattern all over the third panel using a daisy sticker, cosmetic sponge and pink inkpad in the same way as Step one. Position the peel off silver daisy panel in the centre of the sponged background. Add two flat back crystals to the centres of two of the daisies with dimensional glue (see step nine picture).

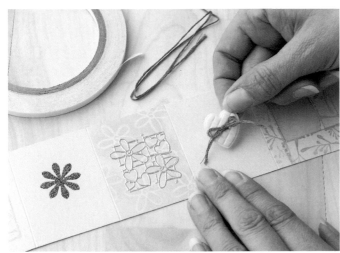

Step seven

Thread a strand of embroidery thread through the heart-shaped button and tie in a bow. Attach to the centre of the next panel with double-sided tape.

Step eight

Cut the photograph 0.6cm (¼in) larger than the frame in the back panel and stick to the back of the booklet using double-sided tape. Stick the teddy bear button to the centre of the stamped front panel with double-sided tape.

Step nine

Fold the booklet up and use double-sided tape to stick the pink ribbon to the back of it, so that you can tie the ends in a bow at the front. Position the concertina booklet on the front of the larger card, remove the tape backing and stick in place.

Weddings

Use this super selection of wedding invitations to spark your imagination: change the colours to fit your own scheme and combine ideas to create your own unique design.

Soft and Sensuous

For a touch of luxury use a white card with gold shimmer and mount a square panel of soft pink mulberry paper centrally. Punch squares of pink and burgundy card and fill with punched daisies and hearts in alternating colours. Flat back crystals add sparkle and dimensional glue is used to highlight the corners of the squares.

Stamped with Love

The purple panel on this pre-scored and folded blank card is made using self-adhesive paper vellum. Use bought tags and add a heart punched from the self-adhesive paper vellum to each one. Add beautiful sheer ribbon to finish the look, and attach the tags with adhesive foam pad.

Simply Stylish

A pre-scored and folded blank card embossed with four squares is the basis of this tasteful invitation. Glue a metal heart in the centre of each square and decorate the corners of the squares with pink dimensional glue.

Gorgeous in Gold

Cream and gold look so luscious together. Glue a gold metal heart to the centre of a small cream square, then attach this to a slightly larger gold square with double-sided tape. Stick to the main card. To finish, add some gold seed beads to gold metallic thread and tie around the fold of the card.

Purple Passion

Cut a heart from self-adhesive purple paper vellum to create the central element of this striking card. Use the same vellum and a small square punch for the borders. Carefully tear a strip of self-adhesive lilac paper vellum and punch three hearts from it and stick over the purple heart. The border and strip embellishments are made from the centres of peel off eyelets.

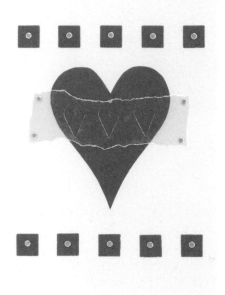

Good Luck Charm

Tear a strip of self-adhesive purple paper vellum and stick down the left side of a soft white card. Top with a strip of patterned vellum using spray adhesive. Wrap purple ribbon around the fold of the card and tie in a bow. Tie some ribbon to a heart and flower charm and attach to the top right of the card.

Celebrations

Here is a selection of cards for all those occasions where a celebration is called for. They look stunning but can be assembled quickly and easily.

Red Roses Valentine

The front and back of this card is covered with a rose design serviette (see page 64). Trace a tag (see page 100–102) and cut out of white card with gold shimmer. Spray mount a torn piece of serviette and add three gold metal hearts and a ribbon bow. Three hearts top right and bottom left finish the card.

Golden Wedding Congratulations

The woven heart is made in the same way as the Woven Wedding Anniversary (see page 50), but for this heart I have used different width strips cut from textured card and paper and even a chocolate foil wrapper. It is mounted to a panel of torn mulberry paper slightly smaller than the gold card.

Coming of Age

Position a peel off one and eight on the front of your card and carefully sponge around the numbers, move the numbers all over the card. Cut a tag from gold card and mount on to black then rust card and add the number 18 using peel off stickers. The car sticker is mounted on the same coloured card. Metal stars are used to embellish the finished design.

Hoppy Easter

Cut egg shapes out of white card then decorate them with a plaid design using the plaid stencil (see page 100–102) and the same technique used for Spring Flowers Easter Card (see page 38). Rubber stamp two Easter bunnies, colour in and cut out. Attach the eggs with double-sided tape and the bunnies with adhesive foam pads.

It's a Girl!

To mark the arrival of a baby girl, rubber stamp the dress on to a square of soft pink card. Stamp again on deep pink and cut out jacket, daisy and trim and stick to the soft pink image. Use a square corner cutter then wrap silver thread around each edge. Mount to your main card and decorate with heart buttons and a gingham bow.

Spooky Hallowe'en

Stamp the cat, spider's web and mouse on to orange card. Stamp and cut the mice and ghost out of white card: colour in and thread wire whiskers through the card. Stamp and cut the bats out of black card and use gel pen for features. Add elements to orange card. Colour in witches hat and use glitter glue on the web. Stick to your main card.

Sentiments

I've created a super selection of cards that are bound to send the right message. Adapt them to the particular occasion you wish to mark, and make them special for you and the recipient.

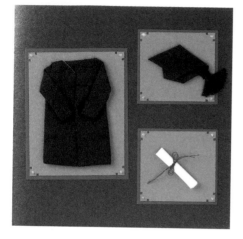

You Passed!

The gown, mortarboard and scroll for this graduation card were bought as ready-made stickers. Mount them on gold card and use a square corner punch and gold dimensional glue to decorate the corners. Mount the gold card on to red card using double-sided adhesive tape, then arrange the three elements on the card.

Girls! Girls! Girls!

If all girls love to shop, this card says it all. Use a handbag rubber stamp over the front of the card and colour in the scarves. Rubber stamp a hat, handbag and shoes on to plain card, colour in and cut out. Mount them on to the blue card with spray adhesive then layer on pink, silver and finally the main card. Add silver eyelet stickers to finish the look.

Celebration Fun

Raised balloon stickers ready-filled with glitter really make this card sparkle. Add curled wire strings to each balloon. Mount the balloons on increasingly larger squares of card in colours that match, then position on a silver card using double-sided adhesive tape.

94

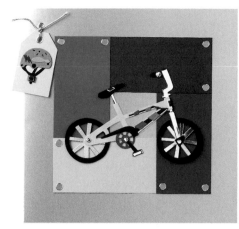

Birthday Boy

Stickers are the basis of this colourful card. Brightly coloured rectangles are stuck in the centre of the card with peel off brads giving the effect of holding the panel on the card. The bike sticker is mounted on top and a bright yellow tag complete with crash hat finishes the card.

In Sympathy

To make this tasteful card a rubber stamp image is coloured in with watercolour pencils then torn from handmade paper before being mounted on to a soft pink card blank. A sheer pink ribbon adds the final touch. Write your special message inside.

New Driver

Use a page from an old road atlas to create the background panel for this congratulations card. Add a rubber stamped car coloured with bright felt-tip pens. Punch a circle from red card and add punched silver keys to make a key fob, then make an 'L' plate and tear it in half. Add shine to the car windscreen and headlights using a dimensional liquid.

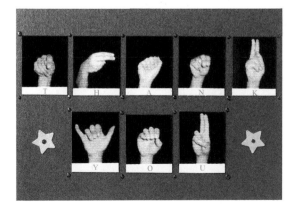

Special Thank You

This card spells out thank you in sign language. I found these pictures on the internet and thought it was a great way to send a message. Each letter tile corner is highlighted with dimensional glue, and the peel off sticker stars balance the design.

Christmas

Christmas cards are such fun to make – all bright colours and cheerful messages to celebrate the festive season. Have fun and really go to town on your own seasonal gift cards.

Sparkly Snowflakes

Using a nine hole aperture blank red card this eye-catching Christmas card is made using the technique explained in Hearts and Flowers Engagement (see page 74). Punched gold snowflakes combine with gold tiny no hole beads and richly contrast with the deep red of the card.

Images of Christmas

Cut six different motifs from a serviette and spray mount each one to a gold square. Decorate each image using glitter glue and dimensional glue and mount them on the front of a purple card.

Snowflake Tag

Cut a panel of snowflake embossed paper vellum slightly smaller than your card and attach using metal snowflake eyelets. Mount a beaded snowflake on a decorative tag and attach to the card with adhesive foam pads. Tie a blue ribbon in the tag to finish.

Seasonal Celebrations

A beaded snowflake is displayed in the single aperture of this ridged white card. Attach it to the inside of the card with an adhesive foam pad. Punch snowflakes out of lilac paper for the border decoration and add a flat back crystal to the centre of each one.

Winter Holly

The plaid background is created using the stencil (see pages 100–102) and technique described in Spring Flowers Easter Card (see page 40). Add green holly leaves and berries made from bright red buttons. Gold thread with seed beads and a snowflake charm is wrapped around the fold of the card.

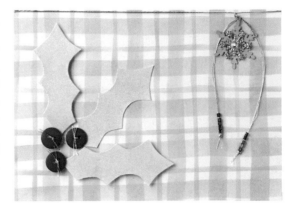

Woven Bauble

Cut a Christmas bauble shape out of tracing paper to fit the size of your card. Weave together strips of festive coloured paper following the technique described in Woven Wedding Anniversary (see page 50), and cut out the bauble shape. Add a pretty ribbon and mount to the card using adhesive foam pads.

Funky Tree Tags

The pocket holding the tags on this unusual card is made from sheer ribbon attached to the card using the zigzag stitch of a sewing machine. Three punched pale green trees are mounted on dark green tags, and bent and shaped wire decorates each tag.

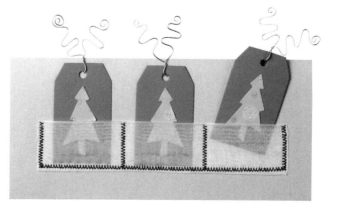

Sayings for Your Cards

Here are some simple messages that you may find appropriate for the cards you have made.

Birthday

Best wishes for a wonderful birthday

Happy Birthday

May all your wishes come true

It's your special day

Best wishes on your special day

May your birthday be as special as you are

May your day be filled with love and laughter

So many candles … so little cake!

Let's party!

General

Get well soon

With deepest sympathy

Just a note

Sending you warmest wishes

Welcome little one

Just for you

Thank you for always being there

You are in our thoughts and prayers at this difficult time

Thank you for your thoughtfulness

Thank you for all you do

Thinking of you

Thank you so much

Inspirational

May all your dreams come true

When all else fails hug your teddy

The sky is the limit

Seize the day

Good luck

Halloween

Trick or treat

Happy Halloween

Trick or treat – give me something good to eat!

Christmas

'Tis the season to be jolly

Season's greetings

May the spirit of Christmas last all year

Cold nose – warm heart

Let it snow

Believe in the miracle of Christmas

Peace Hope Love Joy

Peace on Earth

Joy to you and yours

May all the joys of the season be yours

Merry Christmas

Happy Christmas

Celebrate the season

Shalom

Wedding

Wishing you a lifetime of happiness

For your wedding

Celebrate new beginnings

Best wishes for many happy years together

Love, honour and cherish

Two hearts, one love

Congratulations

Enjoy the moment

Too much of a good thing is wonderful

Sending you all my love

Friends

Friends are kept forever in the heart

Friends are forever

If friends were flowers I'd pick you

You are special to me

I'm here when you need me

Romance

You've captured my heart

You have a special place in my heart

Loves me, loves me not, loves me

Happy Valentines Day

Be my Valentine

My heart belongs to you

You are my sunshine

Special Days

Happy Mother's Day

Happy Father's Day

Happy Easter

Hoppy Easter

Happy anniversary

Templates

Kiddie Cat Birthday – *tag*

New Home Celebration – *tag*

Spring Flowers
Easter Card –
plaid stencils

Spring Flowers
Easter Card –
daisies

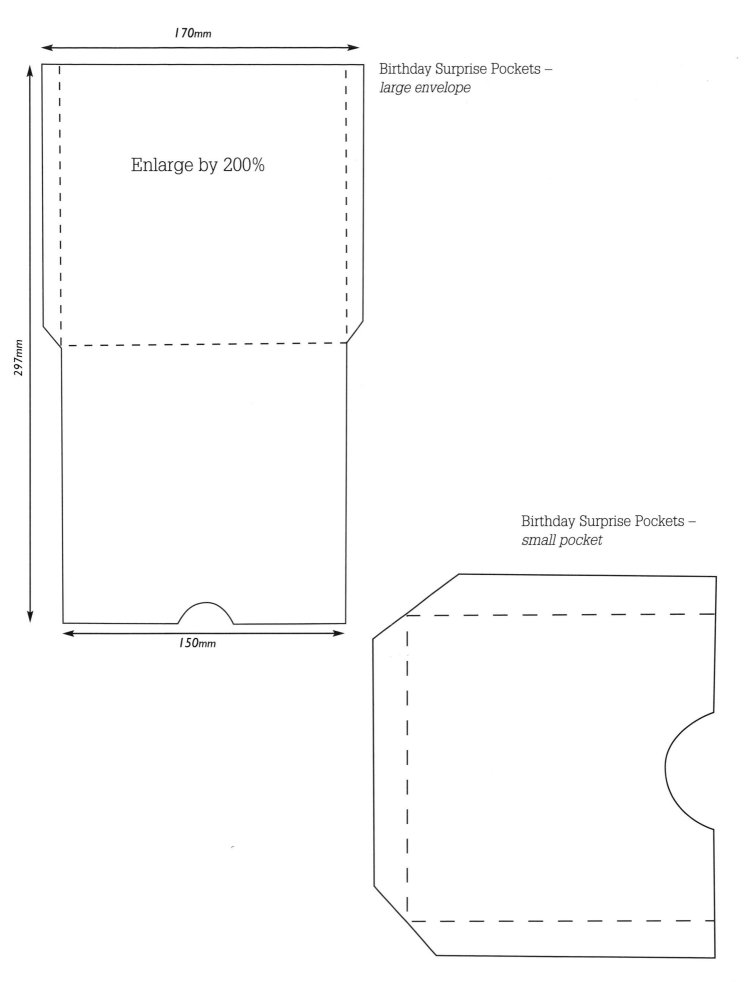

170mm

Birthday Surprise Pockets –
large envelope

Enlarge by 200%

297mm

150mm

Birthday Surprise Pockets –
small pocket

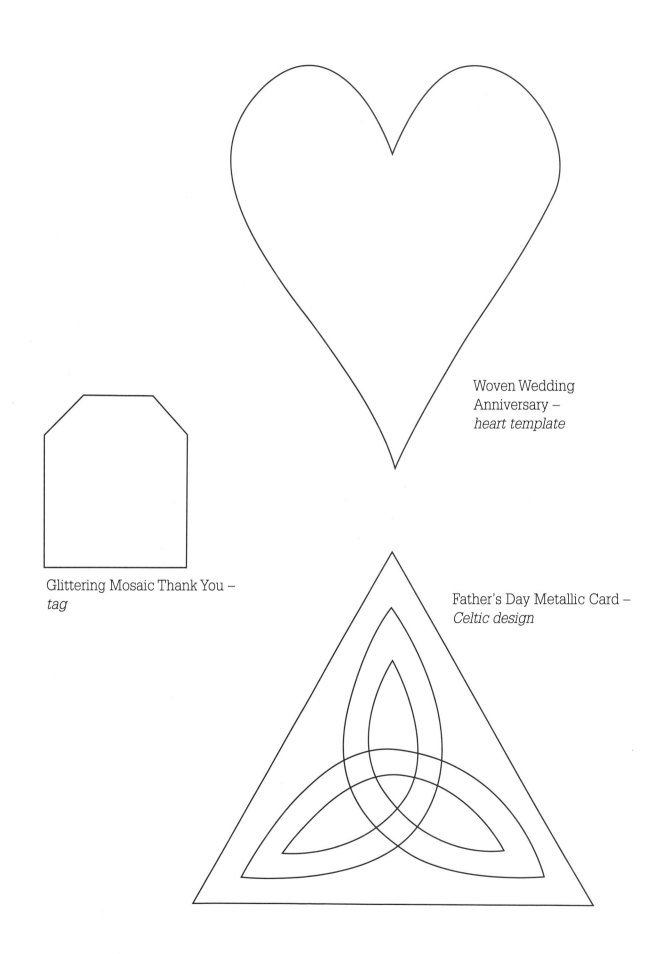

Woven Wedding
Anniversary –
heart template

Glittering Mosaic Thank You –
tag

Father's Day Metallic Card –
Celtic design

Suppliers

UK

The Art of Craft Ltd
248 Shawfield Road
Ash
Aldershot GU12 5DJ
tel: 01252 334855
Mail order service available
A4 double-sided adhesive paper, pegs, serviettes, punches (including mosaic punches), rubber stamps general craft tools and materials

The Craft Barn
9 East Grinstead Road
Lingfield
Surrey RH7 6EP
tel: 01342 836097
fax: 01342 836716
email: info@craftbarn.co.uk
www.craftbarn.co.uk
Mail order service available
Pure copper metal sheets, self adhesive vellum, punches, rubber stamps, general craft tools and materials

Craftwork Cards Limited
Unit 7 The Moorings
Waterside Road
Stourton
Leeds LS10 1DG
tel: 0113 276 5713
fax: 0113 270 5986
email: info@craftworkcards.com
www.craftworkcards.com
Mail order service available
All card blanks, shaped cards, aperture cards and A4 (US letter) sheets of cards, mix up tiny no hole glass beads, ultra-fine glitter, glue pens, dimensional glue, peel off stickers, charms, metal embellishments (hearts, dots and squares), pressed flowers

Crescent Quilling
4 High Street
Shoreham
Kent TN14 7TD
tel: 01959 525799
email: judy@crescentquilling.co.uk
www.crescentquilling.co.uk
Mail order service available
Holographic stickers, peel off stickers, brilliance inkpads, punches, metallic threads, rubber stamps, general craft tools and materials

LA Designs
25 High Street
Milford on Sea
Nr Lymington
Hants SO41 0QF
tel: 01590 644445
Mail order service available
Flat back crystals, peel off stickers, brilliance inkpads, punches, rubber stamps, general craft tools and materials

The London Bead Company
339 Kentish Town Road
London
NW5 2TJ
tel: 0870 203 2323
fax: 0207 284 2062
email: londonbead@dial.pipex.com
www.londonbeadco.co.uk
Seed beads, bugle beads, crystals, general beads and beading equipment

The Scrapbook House
Unit 9
Cromwell Businss Park
Chipping Norton
Oxon OX7 5SR
Tel: 0160 864 3332
www.scrapbookhouse.com
Mail order service available
Novelty buttons, eyelets and tools (hammer, punch and setter), embroidery thread, punches, scrapbooking supplies

Scrap Magic
56 Brighton Road
Surbiton
Surrey KT6 5PL
tel: 0208390 3090
fax: 0208 241 4386
email: debbie@scrapmagic.co.uk
www.scrapmagic.com
Mail order service available
Patterned background papers, vellum papers – plain and printed, heart shaped brads, printed vellum tags, stickers, beaded snowflakes, punches, paper shapers, eyelets and tools (hammer, punch and setter), card and scrapbooking supplies

Xyron UK
19 London Road
Sandy
Bedfordshire
SG19 1HA
tel: 01767 683829
fax: 01767 682224
email: kthomsen@xyron.com
www.xyron.com
Mail order service available
Xyron Machine and cartridges

US

Scrapyard 329
www.scrapyard329.com
Metal embellishment squares and small shapes in assorted colours

Willow Bead
267F South Broadway
Tarrytown
NY10591
USA
www.willowbead.com
Mix up beads, ultra-fine glitter

Acknowledgments

Thank you to Mervyn, Matthew and Owen you are all always so supportive of everything I do. You put up will all the mess, the lack of meals, no clean clothes and me getting stressed out. I could not do what I do without you all. Thank You.

Melanie, you are always there when times get tough – you never fail to amaze me about your belief in my 'commercial' ability. Thank you for all your sparks that light my imagination and help me to create the end results.

I want to say a very BIG thank you to Sue and Richard from Craftwork Cards for supplying all their amazing range of cards for the book and especially for turning my ideas into workable products! You are both so supportive, generous, appreciative, kind and such great friends to have. To everyone, Rose, Simon, Michelle, Julie, Steve and, of course, Andrew and Zara you are all so helpful and friendly. I am so proud to be part of the Craftwork Cards team.

I want to also thank all the shops that have supported me with products for this book. I really appreciate your generosity. Please see page 103 for useful names, addresses and contact numbers.

I have made so many good friends over the years whilst crafting, too many to mention by name, but you have all left your mark and helped me to develop my work one step further. Some special friends include: Maggie, Vesta, Caz, Corinne, Annie, Kim, Jill, Helena, Francoise and Dawn.

Anna – thank you for navigating and taking all the notes down, you made the step by steps much easier to write!

Ginette – your photography of my cards is quite simply stunning and you saved the day! It was a total pleasure working with you and thank you to both you and Stuart for sharing your home and a fabulous lunch!

Carey – you made the text side of my book so easy and it was really great to work with you. It's a shame we never got to meet, but thank you.

Jenny – you have been so helpful and efficient with everything you have done for the book. I really appreciate your help – thank you.

Lisa – I have to say a huge thank you for the excellent design features of this book. You have hit the nail on the head with the layout.

Thank you too, to each and every one of you who buys this book. Without you customers there would be no point to creating more card ideas to share! Enjoy the book and I hope it gets your creativity flowing so that you come up with more ideas yourself.

About the Author

Julie Hickey is a successful card maker, workshop tutor and author. She has been involved in running the Craftwork Card Club by post, which supplies over 2,500 UK members with materials, projects and newsletters. Julie also demonstrates around the UK at all the major craft and rubber stamp shows, and organizes the Rubber Stamp and Card Makers Materials Show in Crawley, West Sussex. She is a regular contributor to *Crafts Beautiful* and *Practical Crafts*, and has appeared on 'Create and Craft' shopping channel on Sky TV. This is Julie's third book, but her first for David & Charles. Julie lives with her husband Mervyn and two sons, Matthew and Owen, in Horley, Surrey.

Index